THE IROQUOIS HUNT

A Bluegrass Foxhunting Tradition

Christopher Oakford & Glenye Oakford

THE History PRESS

Published by The History Press
Charleston, SC 29403
www.historypress.net

First published 2014

Manufactured in the United States

ISBN 978.1.62619. 743.5

To the members—past and present—of the Iroquois Hunt Club

No one knows the trials, tribulations, and difficulties encountered in starting and continuing a hunt.

—John Gourlay, honorary secretary of the Iroquois Hunt

Contents

Acknowledgements

The authors would like to thank the following people for their help in the writing of this book: Lucy Breathitt; Bob and Kathy Brewer; Peter Brook of Baily's Hunting Directory; Charles and Myra Cain; Brownell Alexander Clark; Sayre Combs; Captain Brian Fanshawe, MFH; Norm Fine; Colonel Dennis Foster and Jennifer Strobel of the Masters of Foxhounds Association of America; Bill and Betty Gess; Matthew Harris of the Special Collections Library at the University of Kentucky; Randolph Hollingsworth; Blaine Holloway; Dr. and Mrs. James B. Holloway; Professor James Klotter, Kentucky's state historian; Lilla S. Mason, MFH; Bernard J. Matthys of the American Field Publishing Company; Joan Mayer, MFH; Jerry L. Miller, MFH; Bud Murphy; Cathy Murphy; the staff at the National Sporting Library; Nigel Peel, MFH; Elizabeth Playforth; Elizabeth Preston, archivist at the Thomas Balch Library in Leesburg, Virginia; Judy Sackett, oral history librarian at the University of Kentucky Library; Leonard B. Shouse III; Herb Sledd; Steven Spears; Mrs. Stone of *The Chase* magazine; Dr. Jack van Nagell, MFH; John Venable; and Debbie Young. And in particular, Nancy Dejarnette—descendant of General Roger D. Williams—whose own research was so generously provided to make this book possible.

Introduction

Any writer foolish enough to contemplate producing the history of a foxhunting club is immediately faced with a dilemma. What amount of prior foxhunting knowledge should he or she assume on the part of the reader? To paraphrase P.G. Wodehouse, jump right in, and you risk leaving the newcomer baffled; give a long explanation, and the old hand is likely to be bored. So perhaps the best place to begin this book, if you are unfamiliar with terms such as "giving tongue," "cubbing" and "chop mouthed," is at the end. There, you will find a glossary to help decipher the numerous peculiar words and phrases that litter this history and that necessarily litter every history of fox hunts and foxhunting. On the other hand, if you already know about buttons, Masters and whipping in, you might prefer to skip straight to Chapter 1 and dip your toes into the history of an interesting old institution.

All of this might lead you to ask: why write an introduction in the first place? There are two reasons. In the first place, it is to help the people for whom foxhunting seems vaguely familiar from countless scenes in costume dramas such as *Downton Abbey* and from innumerable paintings and prints and who might in consequence feel tempted to plough straight on. Sadly, I have to warn them that such familiarity is a chimera. At its heart, foxhunting is an esoteric business, full of abstruse language and arcane practices, all apparently rooted in inviolable tradition and governed by occasionally arbitrary rules.

In one sense, this is deliberate and comparatively new. The surface sheen of unfamiliar words and practices was added by Victorian Englishmen, who codified the laws of so many pastimes and who—regrettably—included foxhunting in their rule-making mania. Frequently new to the sport themselves, they liked nothing better than to trip up the unwary beginner with the finer points of etiquette they had themselves only recently invented, in large part to prove their own superiority in knowing them. They did a good job. Like the invention of Christmas—with its set rituals of turkey, tree and snow—it is hard to imagine what hunting was like before the profiteers of the Industrial Age got their hands on it. In fact, it had been content to carry on its way with landowners and guests wearing whatever they felt comfortable in, blissfully unaware of the vital importance of having the correct number of buttons on one's coat. Still, rules, once invented, are hard to do without, and a working knowledge of such terms as "pack," "full cry" and "gone away" is now essential.

But on a far more elementary level, hunting itself is an extremely nebulous business. Why hounds behave as they do, the mysteries of scent and the evasive cunning of foxes and coyotes are all hard to explain, even for professional huntsmen who have spent a lifetime observing such things, making it difficult ever to explain precisely what is happening on a hunt.

My other aim is to clarify what I mean by foxhunting in the first place, which might not be as obvious as it sounds, either to the newcomer or to the old hand. To an Englishman, foxhunting—and, in fact, just the word "hunting"—presents only one scenario: foxes, foxhounds, red coats and horses. To an American, however, it encompasses a whole range of widely differing activities. Naturally, they all involve hounds and foxes (or coyotes), but the method in which the hounds are used and in which the foxhunters pursue their sport can range from night hunting (where the aim is to listen to the hounds chasing their quarry) and field trials (where hunters are sometimes on foot, sometimes on horse, but still mainly intent on listening rather than watching) to mounted hunting in the English manner.

For clarity's sake, when the term "hunting" is used in the following pages, it refers solely to the English style. That, after all, is the ostensible aim of the Iroquois Hunt Club. And I should begin by giving a brief explanation of what happens, or at least what is supposed to happen, on a typical hunt.

One of the best outlines is provided by anthropologist Professor James Howe of the Massachusetts Institute of Technology in his paper "Fox Hunting as Ritual," first published in the journal *American Ethnologist* in 1981.

> *At about midmorning, the participants in the hunt assemble at a crossroads, inn, market, home of a hunt subscriber, or friend of the hunt, or at some*

> *other spot convenient to the fox. Those who actively direct the hounds and hunt the fox include the master, the paid huntsman, and two or more servants known as whippers-in. The hunting field, those who merely follow the hounds, may number anywhere from 20 to 30 up to several hundred. Eventually they all move off toward the woodlot or thicket, known as a covert, where it is presumed the...fox has hidden.*
>
> *There the master and huntsman draw the covert by casting the hounds. The whippers-in and huntsman station themselves at different points around the covert to catch a glimpse of the fox as it bolts the covert. When it does, they give it a few moments lead to avoid chopping it, i.e., catching and killing it right off, before it has shown them some sport. The hounds are put on the trail of the fox; after they have picked up its scent and started off, the signal "Gone Away" is blown on a horn. The riders in the field follow as close behind as they can...many or most galloping as fast as they can, jumping obstacles as they encounter them.*
>
> *For various reasons, the hounds may experience a check, i.e., lose the scent, and those managing the hounds will have to use their skill in casting the hounds so they pick up scent again. If the fox is sighted, the sighters tallyho him to announce the view. Hopefully, the hounds will run down the fox in the open after a long and exciting run, but it sometimes goes to ground...and in many cases it escapes altogether. If time permits, they may then draw another covert.*

There are a few caveats to the above description, chief among which is that in general, American foxhunters aim to chase the fox but not kill it, foxes posing less of a danger to livestock than they do in England. Another important point to remember is that a huntsman is not always a professional. In fact, in many instances, the Master and the huntsman are one and the same person, and the Master hunts his or her hounds (the term "Master" is gender nonspecific) on an amateur basis. And there are often days when hounds do not pick up the scent of a fox or coyote at all. These are known as blank days. But broadly speaking, it gives a good idea of what the English style of hunting involves.

The hunting season generally runs, both in Europe and America, from October until March. The training of hounds takes place during the summer, although young hounds also learn on the job by seeing what older, more seasoned hounds do during a hunt.

The Development of the Sport in England and America

Foxhunting, then, is the art of training a pack of hounds to hunt live quarry, such as fox or coyote, by scent and the sport of riding across country to watch them do it. It has a long history in America. The first hounds that are known to have been imported arrived in 1650, brought from England to Maryland by Robert Brooke of Southampton. The earliest organized hunt was created by Thomas, Lord Fairfax, in the 1740s and 1750s. Fairfax owned vast tracts of land throughout Virginia and was a friend and mentor to George Washington, who was himself a keen foxhunter. The earliest known foxhunting club (or "subscription pack," to use the hunting world's own parlance)—Philadelphia's Gloucester Fox Hunting Club—was founded in October 1766.

Made up of businessmen and professionals (as opposed to aristocrats like Fairfax), who had to pool their resources to pursue their sport (hence the term "subscription"), the Gloucester Fox Hunting Club survived until 1818, with an understandable period of enforced inactivity between 1775 and 1780. The Gloucester hunted two days a week between October and April, crossing the Delaware River to comb the "forests, swamps, and farmlands of southern New Jersey with a pack bred from English foxhounds."[1] Its uniform, chosen by the club in 1774, consisted of "a dark brown cloth coatee with lapelled dragoon pockets, white buttons and frocked sleeves, buff waistcoat and breeches, and a black velvet cap." The pack numbered "about sixteen couple of fleet hounds" and was in the charge of Samuel Morris's slave Old Natt, who was installed as "Knight of the Whip, and became master and commander of all the hounds." Natt was given a salary of fifty dollars a year, a house, a horse and an assistant. Eventually, he saved enough money to buy his freedom.

Traditional wisdom has it that foxhunting provides an excellent preparation for war. In the case of the Gloucester Fox Hunting Club, that certainly seems to have been true. When the Philadelphia First Cavalry was founded, twenty-two members of the Gloucester enrolled in its ranks. And the club's sportsmen had a profound effect on the course of American history. Many were close associates of Washington who, despite their Quaker upbringings, fought in the Revolutionary War. One member, Major Samuel Nicholas, founded the United States Marine Corps (there is a suggestion that the marines' uniforms were modeled on the Gloucester Hunt's livery), and others, such as Captain Samuel Morris and his brother Anthony, fought at Brandywine, Princeton and Trenton.

The Gloucester may, in fact, be the first truly organized subscription hunt anywhere in the world—a delightful irony given the hue and cry that followed the introduction of what was perceived as a wholly English invention to America in the late 1890s and early 1900s.

The Gloucester Fox Hunting Club provides an excellent example of what hunting was like in both England and its American colonies at the midpoint of the eighteenth century. To quote Professor Howe again, "In the 18th century foxhunting was more sedate than now, and emphasis fell more heavily on watching hounds follow a scent…the master of hounds and his companions would go out very early in the morning to pick up its scent, which could be quite cold if the fox had passed that way several hours before. Once the fox had been roused, the chase often proceeded slowly, since the fox generally had a full belly, and the hounds of that era scented better than they ran."

The members of the Gloucester Fox Hunting Club would rise before dawn to pursue their sport, crossing the Delaware by ferry and meeting for an early breakfast before starting the hunt.

The Gloucester's culture also illustrates how closely the two countries remained connected up to the outbreak of war. Many members of the Gloucester were educated partly in England and are believed to have picked up the idea for their own club from watching London professionals and merchants hunting on the outskirts of the city. But over the next century, the sport of foxhunting in England was transformed while the sport in America split into two very different codes.

England

At its most basic level, the development of foxhunting in England was the result of three overlapping and interacting factors: the Enclosure Acts of 1750–1800, the Industrial Revolution (1760–1840) and the generation of sportsmen for whom Hugo Meynell stands as the *beau ideal* and who were determined to improve the sport. The Enclosure Acts—the appropriation and closing off by landowners of land that had, until that point, been in common use—transformed England's landscape. In part, it forced members of the rural poor to look for better paid work in the towns. At the same time, the new patchwork of hedges and fences meant that, in order to follow hounds, hunting men and women now had to have horses that would jump. The movement of large numbers of people to the towns helped fuel the Industrial Revolution, which, in turn, created huge amounts of new wealth, at least for a few. The railways, built toward the end of the period under discussion (1840s), opened up access to the country (and accelerated the process of industrialization at the same time), and the newly enriched industrialists took full advantage by distancing themselves geographically from the sources of their wealth and aiming to ease their entry into the ranks of polite society by emulating the manners and pastimes of gentry. At the same time, traditional foxhunters, led by Hugo Meynell at the Quorn Hunt in Leicestershire, started to hunt later in the day. "The change to…midmorning meets resulted not only in larger fields, but also in faster runs, because the fox had by that time of day digested its meal and because it bolted out of cover with the hounds hard on its heels."[2] In England, foxhunting became popular because it got faster and more thrilling (the result of Meynell and the reconfigured landscape) and because more people had the money to pursue it. Its growing popularity, coupled with the ever-increasing costs of funding a hunt, led to the rise of subscription packs and the gradual decline, or adaptation, of private packs owned by one individual or family. The increase in the speed of foxhunting also necessitated a change in the conformation of the English foxhound, resulting in a lighter-boned, faster animal better able to keep up with the new conditions.

The United States

In the post-Revolutionary United States, hunting developed on markedly different lines. While it was obviously not subject to the forces mentioned above that so altered the sport in England, there were two different factors at work. First, the land was less cultivated than in England and thus harder to navigate, and in many places, it simply was inherently more difficult terrain, regardless of the level of cultivation. And second, the greater independence of the population meant that more people kept small numbers of hunting dogs to help them in their work and to hunt game. This led to the development of a style of hunting in which hounds hunted independent of their handlers. Viewing the hounds at work and interfering directly in their pursuit of the quarry—in the way that an English huntsman might lift the hounds and take them to the next covert if they are having no luck in getting the scent of a fox—is unknown in American hunting of this type. The sport came in listening to the hounds work. American foxhunters became adept at discerning which hound was in the lead by the sound of its cry alone. The sport was also competitive, even if it was also an extremely social activity, and usually there was only admiration—perhaps grudgingly given—for the owners and breeders of the best hounds. Because sportsmen owned fewer hounds and because those hounds worked independently of one another, it was possible to judge which hounds hunted best, anathema in English hunting, where the levelness of the pack is all important. All this is not to say that in the Deep South (and in states such as Kentucky, Maryland, Tennessee and Virginia), landowners with large estates did not continue to have their own private packs and hunt their own land in much the same way Englishmen did prior to the 1760s.

In parts of the North, with its heritage of Puritanism and its penchant for prohibition, foxhunting was in some cases actively banned, despite the example of the Gloucester Fox Hunting Club. But it was in the North that hunting in the English sense—highly organized, formal and governed by a great many rules, albeit some of them only recently invented—at last took hold in America in the early part of the twentieth century. And when it did, it was introduced, for the most part, by newly rich northerners—the American cousins of the industrialists in Victorian England. Men such as J. B. Thomas, Harry Worcester Smith and A. Henry Higginson are the great names still of American hunting. They were all from the North and all rich. And the vast majority of the older hunt clubs that are still in existence in America today were founded between 1900 and 1930.

In fact, of the approximately 160 American hunts active today, only 13 can trace their origins to before the year 1900. This is the history of one of them—the Iroquois Hunt Club, founded in 1880 and the third-oldest such organization in the United States. It is also the history of a hunt founded during that most clubbable of decades, the 1920s. (A total of 45 of the oldest clubs were founded in the '20s alone.) In 1914, the old Iroquois Hunt lapsed into desuetude, and it was not until 1926 that fourteen sportsmen from Lexington, Kentucky, re-founded it, hoping to create an English-style hunt in the heart of the Bluegrass. In its first incarnation, Iroquois reflected the highly idiosyncratic nature of hunting in America at that time. In its second, it conformed more closely to the aspirational spirit of the Jazz Age. In both cases, the men and women who founded it were equally as obsessed with American hunting as they were with its English equivalent. The gap between the two codes led them to some interesting places. Their stories are told here through the history of the club and the sport they loved.

A Note about People, Places and Hounds

Any history is selective, and this, in particular, is just one view of the overarching story of the Iroquois Hunt, or at least the view that has been glimpsed of it from numerous interviews and when wading through hundreds of newspaper articles, journals, letters and photographs. In addition, the amount of space allowed for the story is strictly limited. The consequence of these two facts is that the *dramatis personae* of the following chapters tend to be the men and women who have had the biggest impact on the material items of the hunt, such as the hounds and the club's headquarters, known as Grimes Mill. For the most part, they are the hunt's Masters of Foxhounds, presidents, huntsmen, whippers-in and secretaries. Unfortunately, this ignores a large proportion of Iroquois members, landowners and employees many of whom have contributed immeasurably to the history of the Iroquois Hunt Club through less easily discernable and definable means, such as their presences and personalities. Along with the hounds, they are really the life of the hunt. Hopefully, they will forgive their omission from this story.

While the story follows a broadly chronological narrative, there are aspects of the club's history—such as the confusion over the exact date of its foundation and the development of some of its annual events—that have had to be looked at out of sequence in order to give them full attention.

And for anyone outside of America who might stumble across this book by accident, I should also explain that Kentucky began life as a single, huge county of Virginia. The links between the two states are strong, and unsurprisingly, the families of the men and women who populate the history of the Iroquois Hunt have ties to both places. Williamses, Spearses, Clays, Pursleys and Newcombs—look far enough back into their respective pedigrees, and you will see that they all began in the same few counties of what is now Virginia's prime foxhunting country and moved, usually in the 1780s and 1790s, to Lexington, Paris and Winchester in Kentucky.

Lastly, frequent mention is made of hounds and the various types that are used in hunting. There is a broad divide between English, American and crossbred hounds (literally, a combination of the first two). And I have tried to make the differences between them clear. But there are also a number of subdivisions between the various strains of American hound—such as Maupins, Triggs and Walkers—and in such a general book, the many subtle differences between the various American strains have been ignored. As the noted English Master and huntsman Brian Fanshawe—who also makes an appearance in the following pages—once said, in reality, hounds are all crossbreds.

Chapter 1

Early Days

Had you happened to be wandering through the small town of Lexington, Kentucky, late one Friday afternoon in July 1889—perhaps making your way home after a hard day's toil in one of the town's tobacco or rope factories or breaking your journey south at what was then a convenient stopping point en route—you would have observed what must, even for the time, have been a curious sight. At 5:00 p.m., the region's fashionable young elite, "the most popular young people in Lexington, of both sexes,"[3] started, all of a sudden, to assemble in the center of the town, "the majority on horseback, but a fair sprinkling in vehicles." From all corners, they converged upon Main Street and then, just as inexplicably, made their way en masse to the corner of Gratz Park, a thirty-five-acre site slightly north of the town center that had originally been home to Transylvania College before it was destroyed by fire in 1829. Promptly at 6:00 p.m., they left the town and traveled north up the Maysville Pike, crossing after four miles to Russell Cave Pike and continuing on until they reached the turning for Russell Cave itself. There, after dismounting and seating themselves on cushions and robes spread on the ground, the young people saw a sumptuous feast laid out on a grassy bank at the mouth of the cave. Needing no encouragement, they ate. And as they ate, they were entertained in their "weird surroundings" by Waxey, a well-known local singer and dancer, and his "irresistible band." "The luncheon over, lamps were lighted in the Cave, and the merry party joined in dancing the Virginia Reel, followed by songs and dances by Waxey."[4] At 10:00 p.m., as the light from the guttering lamps flickered on the walls of the cave and on the water of the subterranean spring running through it, the young people of the Bluegrass started for home. By the light of the moon, they made their way slowly back into Lexington, all the way talking excitedly about when they would next be able to do the same thing again.

Five years later, at noon on Saturday, January 27, 1894, residents of the town were offered another unusual sight. A live timber wolf was delivered in a cage to the Adams Express office on Main Street (between Broadway and Mill) in one of the company's wagons. A large crowd, anxious to see the beast, gathered outside. They soon learned that the wolf had been procured to provide entertainment for the Iroquois Hunt. "He was captured in Colorado a few days ago," reported the *Kentucky Leader* the next day, "and is wild as a hawk. Foxes being scarce and uncertain in this section, the club decided to try other game."[5] Three packs of hounds had been assembled, and the following Wednesday, the wolf was to be given a half hour's head start—"for if closely pressed when first released he will depend upon his fighting rather than his running qualities"—after which time the hounds would be unleashed to hunt him.

Like the children of Hamelin, the young ladies and gentlemen of Lexington had in their midst a pied piper. His name was Roger D. Williams, a thirty-two-year-old Kentuckian from Bourbon County, who had traveled extensively in the West. For these young people, dancing by torchlight in the caves of Kentucky, were members of the Iroquois Hunting and Riding Club, founded by Williams just nine years earlier, the forerunner of today's Iroquois Hunt. And while it might seem perverse to begin the history of one of America's oldest fox hunts with the report of a party that had little to do with the chase, it is clear that from its inception, the Iroquois was in equal parts both hunt club and social club and that it was always inextricably linked to the life of the town.

From elegant moonlit picnics to pursuing wolves through the bucolic pastures of the Bluegrass, Roger Williams and the members of the Iroquois Hunt were determined of one thing: that life in Lexington would never be dull.

Uncertain Beginnings: The Founding of the Hunt

In all official accounts of the Iroquois Hunt, two things, at least, are clear: that the club was founded by General Roger D. Williams in Lexington, Kentucky, in the year 1880 and that it was named for Pierre Lorillard's[6] Iroquois, the first American-bred horse to win the English Derby.[7]

And for ninety years, that has been the received wisdom. There are, however, good reasons to believe that the club's origins were not so neatly defined. In fact, there has always been confusion both about its name and the date of its founding.

In its first incarnation, the Iroquois Hunt is believed to have existed from 1880 until 1914, when General Williams was called away on military business and, despite the best efforts of his daughter, Mary Sayre Combs, to keep it going, it was forced to close down. It was revived in the fall of 1926 by a group of local sportsmen, and it wasn't long before the issue of when it *had* actually been founded became one of crucial importance. In 1929, the newly revived club was to be formally recognized by the Masters of Foxhounds Association, hunting's governing body, which required the club to supply the date of its founding. That information would then be written up in the foxhunters' bible, *Baily's Hunting Directory*. And from that point on, every time a Master or huntsman anywhere in the world wanted to find out about Iroquois, he or she would open the pages of his or her *Baily's*, in which it would say, "Iroquois Hunt. Date Founded: ____." But what date should it be?

On January 8, 1929, John Gourlay, secretary of the newly revived club, wrote to Henry Vaughan of the Masters of Foxhounds Association:

> *This afternoon I called on Mrs. Roger D. Williams, and after looking through some of the late General's books I found that the original Iroquois was really started in 1880. Mrs. Lucas B. Combs, the General's daughter, had previously told me that the Hunt was started in 1883, and the fact that it was named for the great race horse Iroquois who won the English Derby in 1881 always led me to believe that she was correct. Mrs. Williams however was very positive about it and said that she was married in 1888 after being engaged to the General for eight years and that he did most of his courting on horseback at the meetings of the Hunt.*

Lest that be taken as conclusive, it is worth noting that by 1929, Mrs. Williams's memory was not uniformly reliable. She had, in fact, been married in 1887.

John Gourlay's point about the date of Iroquois's victory in the Derby is a considerable stumbling block, albeit not an insurmountable one. Why would the club be named Iroquois before the horse won the Derby? As Gourlay goes on to point out in the same letter of January 8, 1929, Iroquois did have a successful two-year-old career in 1880. And it is, of course, possible that Roger Williams named the club before the horse won the race for which he is now remembered. But it was capturing the Derby, the Blue Riband of the Turf, that caught the public's imagination. Iroquois became famous in 1881, not 1880.

And there are other problems to consider, aside from the question of the name. The first public written reference to Williams's club that can be found is in the *Lexington Morning Transcript* of May 5, 1887. A full seven years after the ostensible date of the club's founding. Under the headline "The Lexington Hunting and Riding Club," the paper announced, "The above named club composed of 50 members was organized last week under the most favorable auspices. It had been agitated for the past few years but never given definite shape until the present. The object of the club is health and amusement to be obtained in horse-back riding, fox hunting, and rabbit coursing. Regular meetings will be held at stated times and ere long the music of a pack of hounds will be as familiar as the strains of Trost's band."[8]

A month later, in June 1887, the club held its first major social event, an impromptu series of races for amateur jockeys at the local racetrack. By then, its name had changed to the Iroquois Hunting and Riding Club. Thereafter, the club and its activities were seldom out of the Lexington papers. So another question is why, if Iroquois was founded in 1880 and if its activities were frequently reported on in the local press, is there no reference to it before 1887?

If it was not founded in 1880, what are the possible alternative scenarios? The most widely accepted is that the club grew slowly and emerged from informal gatherings of Williams and his friends, that the name Iroquois was adopted sometime during or after 1881 and that the hunt continued its informal existence until it was officially founded in May 1887. This seems particularly likely, given the tone of the *Lexington Morning Transcript*'s article, which has the ring of a formal announcement from the club, giving a detailed list as it does of the officers and members: "President: Mr. R.D. Williams; Vice President: Miss McDowell; Secretary: James Barr; Treasurer: E.L. Hutchinson."

Indeed, the article even goes on to state the reason for the new club's existence: "By substituting this form of amusement for the death dealing all night dances to which our society of late has become so addicted we expect to see bright eyes, rosy cheeks, and erect forms where now there are too many pale listless faces."

In the Lexington of the mid-1880s, dancing was clearly a serious problem. Six months before the club's 1887 announcement, on an October evening in 1886, the Reverend Robert T. Mathews of the Main Street Church delivered a blistering sermon to his congregation on the evils of dancing. "The number of guests: 50, 100, sometimes 150; the time of the party from 9 o'clock in the evening till the small hours of the morning; the occupation of body, mind, heart—dancing!" he thundered. "This is what our 'society,' so called, is fast coming to. It is possessed with a mania for dancing."

Of course, all this fire and brimstone does raise another possibility, one not wholly inconsistent with the character then and now of the Iroquois Hunt: that the club had already existed for several years and that the announcement in the *Lexington Morning Transcript* of May 5, 1887, was nothing more than an elaborate practical joke designed to tweak the noses of some of Lexington's more puritanical inhabitants. Certainly, Roger Williams and Iroquois never seem to have had any strenuous objection to dancing or late nights, as their parties at Russell Cave confirm. And as one long-standing member of today recalls of attitudes in the 1950s, "I think they [the people in the town] generally thought we rode too fast, drank too much and were having rather too much fun than was good for us."

Sadly, the descendants of General Williams no longer know the whereabouts of the books mentioned in John Gourlay's letter of January 8, 1929. And at this distance in time, proving the exact date on which the Iroquois Hunt Club was founded seems an impossible, not to say unnecessary, task. So, taking the official version of events as the true one, we can begin again. The Iroquois Hunt Club of Lexington, Kentucky, was founded by General Roger D. Williams in the year 1880.

Roger Williams: The Founder of Iroquois

If there is some confusion over the precise details of the Iroquois Hunt's beginnings, there is none over who was its motivating force: General Roger D. Williams—soldier, hunter, businessman, civic leader, organizer and author. At six feet tall and weighing over two hundred pounds, Williams was a physically imposing figure with a personality to match. And although today he might be little remembered, in his own lifetime, he was a person of considerable significance within Kentucky and was widely known nationally, too.

As an officer in the Kentucky National Guard, Williams was in immediate charge of the militia at Frankfort in the aftermath of the assassination of Kentucky's thirty-fourth governor, William Goebel, in February 1900. Through his "tact, judgment, and superb military training"[9] Williams helped prevent the state from sliding into outright civil war, "both sides having great confidence in his impartiality and integrity"—or, as another author puts it, "practically assumed command of the state when Governor Goebel was assassinated."[10] During his thirty-year career with the Kentucky National Guard, Roger Williams rose in rank from lieutenant to brigadier-general, commanding the Second Regiment for fifteen years, during which time he was frequently called on "to suppress mountain feuds, night riding, and other acts of lawlessness."

His services were also in demand from people outside the state. In 1898, his friend Theodore Roosevelt asked him to supply a contingent of one hundred Rough Riders from Kentucky for the Spanish-American War, though the war was over before the troop could mobilize. And in 1918, when he was declared unfit for active service, he traveled to France nonetheless to serve in the headquarters of the First Army following America's entry into the First World War.

Williams's fame as a hunter was even more widespread. As fellow hunter Theodore Roosevelt wrote in *The Wilderness Hunter*, "[He] more than any other American is entitled to speak upon hunting big game with horse and hound." He and Roosevelt were charter members of the Boone and Crockett Club, which did much to assist the conservation of the national parks, in particular Yellowstone. And Williams also helped found the National Foxhunters Association.

It was a life lived in the public sphere and, to a large extent, dedicated to public service, an attitude inherited directly from the progenitor of the Williams line in America—Roger Williams,[11] the founder of Rhode Island.

Over the course of the following century, the descendants of Roger Williams of Rhode Island gradually moved south, settling first in Frankfort County, Virginia, and then moving in the 1790s—in the time of Roger Williams's great-grandfather—to Bourbon County, Kentucky, where, on August 28, 1856, the future General Roger D. Williams was born, the eldest child of Benjamin Franklin Williams and Mary Gates Massie.

The Williamses clearly inherited their ancestor's independence of mind, and they added to it a capacity of their own to stay on good terms with their neighbors. General Roger D. Williams's grandfather Major George Williams served for "twenty consecutive years without a single defeat in both houses of the legislature [of Kentucky], was a delegate to the constitutional convention of 1849, became a champion of the new constitution party… and some years before The War freed his slaves and was an uncompromising Union man during the strife which followed the election of Lincoln."

And the family was sufficiently pro-Union to decamp to Chicago during the Civil War, which erupted within five years of his birth (a large part of Williams's childhood was spent there and in Cincinnati). It is not known exactly when the family returned to Kentucky. But the next sighting of Roger D. Williams occurs in 1872, when he enrolled in Transylvania College, at that time "the youngest student ever to have matriculated the institution."[12] In 1874, he left Kentucky again to travel for a few years in the West, returning in 1879 to establish the Kentucky Copper Works and Iron Foundry, and thereafter Lexington remained Williams's base of operations for the rest of his life.

The impression one gets from such accounts is of a person born into the elite who moved smoothly along rails laid down by preceding generations; someone with energy and intelligence but perhaps rather stolid and conservative; an outdoorsman: part soldier, part hunter. And certainly he seems to have been happiest when engaged in some form of activity. A few days before he died in 1925, he cancelled a long-planned trip to the National Field Trials, saying, "I have a game leg and would not be able to ride. I have no use for rocking-chair hunting" and opting instead to go to work where he would be of some use.

But such a description is only half the story and does little to explain the influence he exerted over the gilded youth of the Bluegrass for a period of thirty-five years. In fact, like many other leaders of his era—including his friend Theodore Roosevelt—Roger Williams was also addicted to adventure and was skilled at writing about his experiences. Upon leaving Kentucky University, as Transylvania College was then known, at an early age, he worked for two years as a clerk before the lure of excitement in the West proved irresistible.

In 1874, Roger Williams left Lexington and headed for the Black Hills of Colorado,[13] eventually ending up in Deadwood, from where he sent a report home on conditions in the Black Hills that was published in the *Lexington Morning Transcript* in 1876. Twenty years later, he wrote a fuller account in "Old Times in the Black Hills," which was published by the Boone and Crockett Club in the book *American Big-Game Hunting*:

> *In the spring of '75 I found myself one of a party of six occupying a rude but strongly fortified stockade on French Creek, in the Black Hills, almost under the shadow of Calamity Peak, and not far from where Custer City was afterward built.*
>
> *I had left Denver the previous fall, quite a tenderfoot…wanting "strange countries for to see," I determined to join a party that I heard was outfitting*

> *at Cheyenne to go into the Black Hills upon a hunting and prospecting tour, under the guidance of old California Joe, one of the most noted scouts and hunters in the West. At this time the presence of gold in the Black Hills was hardly known, and the country, being an Indian reservation, had not even been explored by white men, or surveyed by the government.*

After eventually locating the party, Williams explained:

> [I] *soon rode into their camp, after dark, in a blinding snow-storm. My welcome was anything but cordial. They regarded my story that I, a tenderfoot, had ridden through from Denver in four days to join them as suspicious, and believed, as I afterward ascertained, that I had been sent out from the post to spy upon their movements. During the argument that followed my arrival and proposition to join them, I observed a large, powerfully built man, dressed in buckskin, seated apart from the rest. He was eating the meat from a section of ribs he had scraped out from among the coals and ashes. He took no part in the conversation until, in answer to a question, I stated that I was a Kentuckian. At this he rose and settled the matter by saying that if I was a Kentuckian he would vouch for my honesty of purpose, and that I would stand fire in the scrimmages that we were certain to have with the Sioux. This was California Joe, who for years had been chief of scouts with General Custer. He afterward informed me that he was from near Danville, Kentucky, that his name was Mose Milner, and that he had gone west in the forties.*

Williams spent the next few years, those of his late teens and early twenties, as a prospector and hunter. He also joined the Black Hill Rangers[14] under the leadership of Captain Jack Crawford.[15]

On several occasions, the Black Hills almost proved his undoing. According to Custer City resident Sidney J. Cornell, in 1876, Martha Jane Canary, more popularly known as "Calamity Jane," "tried to stab Roger D. Williams in a Custer store because he laughed at her."[16] He also put his literary skills to good use, becoming a war correspondent for the *San Francisco Chronicle* and the *Denver Tribune* and reporting on the Battle of Little Big Horn for those papers. He continued to write about his experiences hunting and prospecting the Black Hills for the rest of his life.

But like many of the personalities drawn to the West at that time, Roger Williams was not simply addicted to life in the wild. He was also an entertainer. Of his immediate friends, Crawford and California Joe became noted public speakers once their scouting days were over, while Buffalo Bill—a great friend of Crawford's—took his Wild West show on the road. Another friend, Wild Bill Hickok (killed in Deadwood in 1876), was well known as an amateur actor but was admittedly more famous for his love of indiscriminate slaughter. In 1877, tired of prospecting and scouting, and perhaps tired also of fraternizing with a group so noted for their homicidal tendencies, Roger Williams moved to San Francisco and joined the California Theatre Company. He stayed for two years, appearing alongside actors Joe Jefferson, Thomas Keene, Fannie Davenport and, most famous of them all, Edwin Booth, the brother of John Wilkes Booth.[17] In the summer of 1881, four years after he and Williams appeared together on stage in San Francisco, Booth was on tour in England. And while his former colleague Williams was in Lexington—possibly naming his new hunt after America's latest sporting hero, Pierre Lorillard's Iroquois—Booth was at Epsom in person watching the horse make its historic run.

The love of entertaining remained with Roger Williams, as did his love of adventure and writing. Every spring for the rest of his adult life, he would depart, unannounced, for the Black Hills, leaving his wife to run the iron foundry. Perhaps it was these qualities of restlessness and imagination and the love of entertaining that prompted him to plan jaunts such as the moonlit picnic at Russell Cave and to see no obstacle to importing whatever species of animal he wanted to hunt, no matter how dangerous and brutal it might seem to modern sensibilities. Put simply, like many of the best and most successful huntsmen, Roger Williams knew how to put on a show.

Lexington in 1880

In 1879, Roger Williams returned to Lexington and, with the financial backing of his father, established the Kentucky Copper Works and Iron Foundry, situated where Thoroughbred Park stands today, which at that time was on the edge of the town. For many years, it was the only iron foundry in Central Kentucky, and Williams prospered throughout the economic boom of the 1880s. Eight years later, he married Minnie Lyle Sayre, the youngest daughter of Ephraim Danforth Sayre, who "for many years had the oldest and best known private bank west of the Alleghenies."[18] In due course, the couple had two children—Roger Williams Jr. and Mary Sayre Williams.

The town Williams returned to in 1879 was small, with a population of just under 20,000—especially when compared to its neighbors Louisville (123,000) and Cincinnati (255,000)[19]—and was both determinedly set in its ways and surprisingly keen to augment change.

One example of its recalcitrance is the debate over changing the system of time. In the early 1880s, as railroads became increasingly common, many American towns and cities agreed to change from using solar time to a uniform system to allow consistent arrival and departure times to be posted everywhere. (The advent of railways had precipitated a similar change in Europe.) Lexington, however, was extremely reluctant to change and obdurately held out until the early 1890s. As local historian Randolph Hollingsworth pointed out in *Lexington: Queen of the Bluegrass*, "The farmers and grocers in the city halted an attempt by the mayor to change all the city clocks to the standard time used by the railroad companies and most other cities since 1883." The new time was only adopted after "a lecture by Mrs. Dudley Short of the Women's Club of Central Kentucky [convinced the] city council members that the traditional solar time (or God's Time) was also man-made and that the city clocks...should all be turned back twenty-two minutes to conform with the rest of modern America."[20]

At the same time, however, the town also engaged in a large number of public improvements, and this lent it a surprisingly multicultural feel. Italian workmen, who spoke little or no English, were brought in to install a public system of waterworks, and although the German population was small, it had a disproportionately large impact, with many German clubs established and even a page in the local paper printed in German. The town was quick to incorporate innovations, such as street railways and telephone lines—as people were connected to the network, their names and phone numbers were published on the front page of the newspaper. Culturally, too, Lexington residents were eager to avoid any isolation their geographical position away from the main urban centers might impose, and by the 1880s, they had "a new Opera House, two quadrille bands, a musical society, and a theater."[21]

Unsurprisingly, sport also played a major role in the life of the town. In 1828, a group including Henry Clay purchased a sixty-five-acre site at the eastern edge of the town (just north of where present-day Midland Avenue and Winchester Road meet) and built a mile-long dirt racetrack known as the "Association track."

The main industry was still agriculture: tobacco, livestock and hemp. Transport was still by horse, as the records of Iroquois parties attest, with frequently as many as sixty guests traveling up the Maysville Pike on horseback and in a variety of carriages. In fact, the 1880s was the heyday of stagecoach travel all across Kentucky, and in 1882, a system of mule-drawn streetcars was introduced. But change was rapid, and by 1890, the mule-drawn cars had been replaced by electric ones, and stagecoaches had been replaced by a system of railways with Lexington as the central point of several lines.

When Williams returned in 1879, Lexington was celebrated both as a city of culture and a frontier town. Kentucky's state flag, which depicts two men—one dressed in city clothes, the other in buckskins—shaking hands, reflects this duality. And in his combination of urbanity and ruggedness, Williams personified the qualities of his hometown.

Early Activities of the Hunt

Whether or not Williams's Iroquois Hunting and Riding Club had been active in the early part of the 1880s, when it finally made its first public appearance, it did so with a bang. The race meet for amateur riders held at the Association track in June 1887 was an instant success. Under the headline "A Rare Afternoon's Sport," the *Kentucky Leader* article of June 12, 1887, begins, "In the annals of Lexington there has never been an event that has afforded more pleasure, more enjoyment, than the races, impromptu as they were, that took place at Lexington Race Track yesterday afternoon."

General Williams was the starter (at six feet in height and weighing over two hundred pounds, he was not ideal jockey material). But many members of the new club took a more active part. And from 1887 on, Iroquois held at least one meet a year and often two—one in the summer and one in the fall. The race meets were hugely popular, regularly attracting crowds of several thousand, and through them Iroquois became one of the leading providers of sporting entertainment for the community as a whole—even if the Association track did not provide nineteenth-century Lexington residents with quite the same viewing opportunities their modern-day counterparts enjoy at Keeneland today.

As the *Thoroughbred Record* reported in 1900, "The hemp crop covering the entire center field of the Kentucky Association track at Lexington has mounted to its height of eight, ten, twelve, feet. From the grandstand it is impossible to see any of the poles which mark the furlongs and half-furlongs in the back-stretch. One of Dillard Hill's horses is reputed to have worked six furlongs in 1:16½. The timers were doubtless in a balloon, for it is manifestly impossible for a man, unless at a great elevation, to see a horse at the three-quarter pole."

Racing apart, there was a plethora of other activities. The winter was devoted chiefly to hunting. Fox, raccoon and rabbit were all fair game, and there were also drag hunts, in which no live quarry was hunted but instead a trail was laid for the hounds and hunters to follow using a rag soaked in the scent of a fox. And each spring, Iroquois members were bidden to General Williams's house on the corner of Main Street and Ashland Avenue to help plan a program of summer rides, polo and picnics. Members received handwritten invitations in the mail, and the date and time of the meeting was then announced in the Lexington press.

One of the main locations for drag hunts was Solomon Van Meter's[22] house, Shenandoah Hall, on Bryan Station Pike. A daughter of the house, Margaret Van Meter Capers, left a brief description of what they were like, written on the back of a photograph:

> *General Williams had the hounds in a crate on a spring wagon and released them in the front yard. Our fox slept on a sheepskin in his coop. Father would tie a small rope around the sheepskin, dip it in a tub of water, put the houseboy on a horse and tell him the route to drag the skin around our farm—starting back of the house crossing over near the parkway—over the pike—over the front pasture to the Hume's then back near Johnnie Marrs* [now Clarkland Farm] *and home—several miles. All the ladies are on side saddles.*

Margaret Van Meter modestly forbore to mention her starring role in the hunt, but the event was also captured for posterity in the Sunday morning edition of the *Kentucky Leader*: "The run was three, or four miles across country, Miss Margaret Van Meter coming in first, Mr. Robert McClintock second, and Miss Mary Sayre Williams [General Williams's daughter] third." After the hunt, the party went en masse to dinner at the country club at nine o'clock before returning for a raccoon hunt. A midnight supper by a bonfire in the woods followed, and "the happy party reached home about 2 o'clock."

If hunting was the preoccupation of winter, the highlights of summer were the rides to Russell Cave. At least half a dozen descriptions of such trips survive in the archives of the Lexington newspapers. They all follow the same pattern. Iroquois members—summoned by postal card—would set off from Gratz Park in the late afternoon or early evening. The cave, one of a series of limestone caves surrounding Lexington, had been a popular meeting place for generations. Cassius Clay had held a political rally there, which had descended into violence (a not unusual occurrence) in 1843. On many occasions, the entertainment for Iroquois' parties was provided by Waxey[23] and his band—an enormously popular local group of singers, dancers and musicians.

The route out to Russell Cave led Iroquois members past Gentry Place on Russell Cave Pike, the home of "General" William Gentry.[24] Also known as "Jack Rabbit" on account of his owning the only jack rabbit park in Lexington, Gentry was considered by his peers as "a man of originality and somewhat eccentric."[25] He was named for General William Harrison and from childhood was known to everyone as "General." He was a keen participant in the hunt during its first incarnation from 1880 to 1914, hosting numerous fox, raccoon and rabbit hunts.

General Gentry provided entertainment not only for Iroquois but for the whole town as well. On January 1, 1902, he and his son, Lawrence, held a jack rabbit and fox chase that was reported by the *Kentucky Leader*:

> *Shivering and shaking from the blasts of a cold east wind, fully 1,500, white and colored, including the usual complement of small boys, assembled at the fair grounds this morning to witnes...a jack rabbit and fox chase given by Gen. W.H. Gentry and his son, Mr. Lawrence Gentry of Gentry Place.*
>
> *After parading through the city on his fine charger, Gen. Gentry, attired in his handsome hunting suit, blowing his hunting horn and looking every inch a hunter, accompanied by his son, a wagon load of Beagle hounds, two jack rabbits and a fox, appeared on the scene in all his glory.*

What followed was a fairly inglorious rabbit hunt by an assortment of ten beagles and other hounds. The day was so cold that the crowd left before the fox could be chased but not before "voting Gen. Gentry a royal entertainer."

The picture of the early Iroquois Hunt that emerges is of a small coterie of closely related families and their friends, who formed, in effect, the young social elite of the town. The names of participants and guests visiting from out of town were meticulously recorded by the papers, and it is possible to build up a picture of who the most stalwart members of the club were at that time. Chief among them were the Williamses, the Prestons, the Graveses, the Breckinridges, the Van Meters, the Gentrys, the McDowells, the Haggins and the Clays.

Just how closely connected—and well connected—the group was is illustrated by two of the most regular participants in Iroquois's events: Nettie McDowell, the vice-president of the club in 1887, and Madge Breckinridge,[26] wife of the *Lexington Herald*'s editor, Desha Breckinridge. Nettie and Madge were sisters, the great-granddaughters of Kentucky's great statesman, Henry Clay, and had been brought up at the Clay family home, Ashland, which was just outside the town. And although there is no suggestion that Iroquois was ever anything other than a social club, nonetheless, to the extent that some of the members were concerned with politics, they were for the most part socially progressive, albeit in a strictly patrician sense. Williams was a Republican and a supporter of Roosevelt, a proponent of trust busting, conservation and welfare. Madge Breckinridge was a leader of the women's suffrage movement, and her husband, Desha—descendant of the creator of public education in Kentucky—edited and published the more liberal of the two Lexington newspapers.

Despite the same names appearing again and again in the lists, however, collectively, the members of Iroquois seem not to have been solely concerned with their own entertainment but hopeful of providing fun for all, as was the case with the races at the Association track. In 1890, the *Kentucky Leader* reported, "The time of year is arriving for out of door sports, and the Iroquois Riding and Hunting Club of this city will take advantage of it by organizing a Polo Club." Naturally enough, the original members of the polo club were to be drawn from Iroquois, but as the report made clear, others who wanted to join in were welcome.

Above: Pierre Lorillard's Iroquois with Fred Archer up, winner of the 1880 Epsom Derby. *Bridgeman Images*.

Right: General Roger D. Williams, MFH, the founder of the Iroquois Hunt. *Mr. Sayre Combs*.

General Williams and Ed, runner-up in the 1914 National Field Trials. *Mr. Sayre Combs.*

Opposite: William Bonnie Stone and Josephine Stone. *From* The Chase *magazine*.

Mrs. Lucas B. Combs, General Williams's daughter. *Mr. Sayre Combs.*

Chapter 2

American Hounds for American Foxes

To Hunt in the English Style?

So far back as 1880 the late General Roger D. Williams recognized the need for a well-established Hunt. He had inherited the love of the sport from his father, grand-father, and great grand-father, all of whom were native Kentuckians and had maintained packs of foxhounds, so gathering some friends about him, he founded the Iroquois Hunt in which he served as Master so long as there were supporters to ride with him.
—The Chase, *1927*

Roger D. Williams's aim in establishing the Iroquois Hunting and Riding Club was to provide the sportsmen and women of the Bluegrass with a properly organized hunt. To some, such as the author of *The Chase*'s 1927 article quoted above, that meant the English style of hunting. But whether Williams, in fact, ever intended to introduce the full rigmarole of English foxhunting to Kentucky is debatable. Certainly, however, when he returned home in 1879, Williams had in mind something more organized than, and different from, what existed already. At first, it seems, he found it hard to convince Kentucky's sportsmen and women of the value of his idea, as the article in *The Chase* explains:

> *On several occasions Gen. Williams told me how cautiously he had been compelled to go ahead with his Hunt because of the rather provincial attitude which some friends and good sportsmen took toward the venture, on the supposition apparently that hunting in this way was un-American, or unmanly, or something of this kind, though their own forefathers in England, in Virginia, and even in Kentucky followed the English methods in hunting so far as they could, and attempted to ride as close to the pack as it was physically possible in the new country of unfelled forests and unfordable streams.*

The skepticism was due, in part, to the predominance of a form of hunting traditional to Kentucky and as different from English hunting as could be: night hunting. Night hunters hunt fox—or rather, their hounds hunt fox, the night hunters themselves having no participation in the chase at all. As the name implies, the action takes place at night, so watching hounds work—the primary aim of mounted or English hunting—is almost impossible. The night hunter's pleasure lies in listening as the hounds work. And unlike English hunting, the aim is not to kill but to chase. The natural consequence of this style of hunting was the creation of a hound that was highly independent and able to work alone, without the need for human supervision and without the aid of a surrounding pack of other hounds. Such hounds were smaller and lighter than their English counterparts in order to be able to work their way through thickets and briar and to be better able to stand up to traveling over long distances.[27] Above all, the hounds had two attributes that English hounds lacked, according to their American critics: voice and nose. Night hunters are adept at telling which hound is in pursuit of the fox from the sound of the hound's cry alone. So a hound that would speak loudly and often was preferred. And in the difficult terrain over which the American hounds hunted, they needed to be able to pick up the cold scent of a fox that might have been in the vicinity several hours before.

To people used to such an independent and individualistic type of hunting, the full panoply of the English style, with red coats, top boots, silk hats and hunt servants, must have seemed indescribably strange. But in Williams's time, the local population was not simply skeptical of effete English manners. In the 1880s, foxhunting itself was an activity looked upon with grave suspicion by respectable Kentuckians, according to John Fox's *Bluegrass and Rhododendron: Outdoors in Old Kentucky*:

> *But fox-hunting got into disrepute. Hunting in Southern fashion requires a genius for leisure that was taken advantage of by ne'er-do-wells and scapegraces, who used it as a cloak for idleness, drinking, and general mischief. They broke down the farmer's fences, left his gates open, trampled his grain, and brought a reproach on the fox-hunter that is yet alive.*

Fox's book was published in 1901 and records the author's experiences hunting with many notable Kentucky foxhunters, including Iroquois and General Williams, in the mid- to late 1890s. In it, Fox goes on to explain that families such as the Clays of Bourbon County and the Walkers of Garrard County gradually began to restore the reputation of foxhunting until, by the time Fox's book was published, the sport—which, according to Fox, had hitherto been done individually—was becoming fashionable:

> *Now, hunt clubs are being formed. Chief among them are the Bourbon Kennels, the Strodes Valley Hunt Club, and the Iroquois Club, the last having been in existence for ten years. This club does not confine itself to foxes, but is democratic enough to include coons and rabbits.*

Even here, though, it seems it was too much to expect any kind of uniformity of approach. As Fox recounted in his experiences of field trialing and night hunting in Bath County:

> *There were fox-hunters from Maine, the Virginias, Ohio, and from England; and the contrasts were marked even among the Kentuckians who came from the Iroquois Club, of Lexington, with bang-tailed horses and top-boots; from the Strodes Valley Hunt Club and Bourbon Kennels, who disdain any accouterment on horseback that they do not wear on foot; and from the best-known fox-hunting family in the South, who dress and hunt after their own way, and whom I shall call Walkers because they are never seen on foot.*

The Walkers were, indeed, the first family of foxhunting in Kentucky, which by the late 1880s had become the acknowledged capital of the American foxhound breeding world. As an article in *The Chase* magazine of 1925 explained, "Wilson Tisdale from Tennessee was one of the first to recognize the commercial value of the Kentucky hound. He brought up quantities of mules every year, drove them South and sold them in New Orleans. From there he brought word of the great demand for hounds to hunt deer in the brakes of the far South. It was between seventy-eight and eighty years ago that he took the first shipment of hounds ever known to have been 'traded and trafficked' from Kentucky. He is said to have bought every spare hound in the Counties through which he passed." Through Tisdale and people like him, the fame of Kentucky's hounds, like that of its Thoroughbreds and its whiskey, spread far and wide.

Other states had many fine strains of American hounds, many of which were named for the families or individuals who bred them. Virginia could boast of the Bywaters, Georgia of the Birdsong and Tennessee of the Wild Goose. But besides the Walker hound, Kentucky could also claim Triggs, Julys, Maupins, Williamses and Smiths. Chief among them, though, remained the hounds of the Walker family. Perhaps no other family in American foxhunting has been as revered. In *Bluegrass and Rhododendron*, John Fox tried to convey their mystique: "No Walker reaches the age of sixteen without being six feet high. There were four with us, and the shortest was six feet two and weighed 185 pounds. They wore great oilskin mackintoshes, and were superbly mounted on half thoroughbreds."

Despite their fearsome appearance, the Walkers were God-fearing, soft-voiced and gentle. The family held much of their property in common, except their hounds. Fox noted, "No Walker's dog will follow any other Walker, or come to his horn."

They would hunt at any time of day, but their preference was for night hunting. Fox wrote, "The Walkers hunt chiefly at night. The fox is then making his circuit for food, and the scent is better. At night the hounds trot at the horses' heels until a fire is built on some ridge. Then they go out to hunt a trail, while the hunters tie their horses and sit around telling fine stories until one steady old hound gives tongue. Then they listen to the music."[28]

Coupled with their prodigious appetite for hunting and their undoubted skill, what made the Walkers stand out was their judicious breeding of English bitches to a native dog hound called Tennessee Lead that resulted in a strain of hound hard to beat on red fox. So many tales are told of Tennessee Lead that it is frankly impossible to reconcile them all into one coherent and accurate account. By common consent, it was the Walkers' close friend and neighbor George Washington Maupin of Madison County, Kentucky, who had first found Lead. (He is reputed to have bought him from, or been given him by, a stock driver who happened upon a fox hunt on the Kentucky/Tennessee border and who promptly stole the leading hound and brought it to Madison County.) Lead's importance stemmed from the fact that he is believed, at least by some, to have been the first hound to have caught or run to ground (again, depending on which of the myriad stories you believe) the first red fox in Kentucky. In 1850, there were no red foxes in Kentucky. Foxhunters bred their hounds to chase gray fox and deer. But in the early years of the decade, red foxes started migrating into the state, and the hunters suddenly found their hounds were chasing something they were unable to catch. Coming from Tennessee, Lead was used to red fox. Lead's fame among foxhunters spread quickly, and he was used so extensively as a stud dog that his name is practically ubiquitous in the pedigrees of all American hounds. But the Walkers determined to try outcrossing him with English hounds, which they had been importing regularly for several decades. The progeny proved so exceptionally able that, over time, the new strain of Walker hounds became the overwhelming favorites of American night hunters and successive Masters and huntsmen of the Iroquois Hunt.

Night hunting was also competitive. Whereas English foxhunting relied on packs of hounds, night hunters used individuals. And this meant that hounds could be judged against one another and opinions given about which was best; this was anathema to the English, who felt no single hound should stand out. As John Fox pointed out, "The Englishman wants his pack uniform in color, size, tongue, and speed—a hound that is too fast must be counted out. The Kentuckian wants his hound to leave the rest behind, if he can." Inevitably, this led to direct competitions, known as field trials, which were held during daylight hours so hounds could be seen and judged.

Equally inevitably—and somewhat ironically for a person known today as the father of an English-style hunt—Roger Williams was also a central figure in field trial development.[29] Although field trials had been held since the mid-1850s, it was the formation of the National Foxhunters Association in 1893 that first provided a recognized framework for such events. Williams was a charter member of the organization and the association's keeper of the Stud Book.

The first National All Age Championship was held at Olympia, near Owingsville, Kentucky (about fifty miles west of Lexington), in 1894.[30] No decisions were reached due to dry weather, and it seems likely that this is the event described by John Fox in *Bluegrass and Rhododendron*: "That was the trouble, for hunters say there is never rain to drop when the moon is tipped that way. So the field trials had been given up; the country was too rough; and…the local sportsmen…held the effort in disfavor." He continued and explained where the event was to have taken place: "The hunters were noisily coming and going from the little hotel that was a famous summer-resort in the Bath County Hills forty years ago, and, once owned by a great Kentuckian, was, the tradition goes, lost by him in a game of poker."[31]

Despite all the Kentuckian teeth-sucking over one of their own returning with such foreign ideas, it is clear that General Williams did eventually succeed in converting at least a few of his friends to participate in his dangerously cosmopolitan style of hunting. A fleeting reference in an account he wrote for the *American Field* magazine in February 1894 gives an idea of what it was like: "When I state that on our fox hunt Judge Perry broke a leg, that Mr. Van Goode met with the same fate on the wolf chase, and that one of our members was killed a few years ago, you will agree with me that fox-hunting in Kentucky is not without a spice of danger."

But unfortunately, in all the articles written about the club that appeared in Lexington's newspapers and national sporting journals between 1880 and 1914, there are almost no references to foxhunting. (In the same period, there are dozens of pieces about rabbit hunts, racoon hunts, picnics, races, dances and polo.) The references that do exist relate almost exclusively to field trials, as in John Fox's account in *Bluegrass and Rhododendron*. If Williams's aim was to create an English hunt, he has left us few clues as to what it was like.

We do know, if *The Chase*'s article of 1927 is to be believed, that the hunts probably took place to the south of the town, around a small village called Athens: "The country hunted by him around Athens, laying ten miles from Lexington, was then for the most part rolling blue grass pasture land, enclosed with rail fences and stone walls. The existence of many extensive breeding establishments then, as now, prevented hunting nearer to Lexington, but General Williams clearly saw the future for such a Hunt in the heart of the Blue Grass."

Athens (pronounced with a long "a" by natives to the region) was also home to the man who became General Williams's most trusted aide, William Bonnie Stone. As his obituary in *The Chase* magazine recorded, "William Bonnie Stone was born in Madison County, Kentucky, in 1872. He passed his entire life hunting and breeding foxhounds exclusively. At an early age he moved to Fayette County where he became associated with the late General Roger Williams under the kennel name of Rookwood Kennels.[32] This kennel was most successful in competition on the bench and in the field."

Stone and Williams's association lasted from the 1890s until the General's death in 1925, and Stone is often referred to as General Williams's huntsman, the implication being that Stone was also the huntsman for the

Iroquois Hunt. There is, apparently, no documentary evidence to confirm this, but certainly Bonnie Stone was a dedicated night hunter. Hunt member Charlotte Pursley was to recall that in the late 1920s, when the club was just starting again, Iroquois's members spent many nights sitting by fires on the hills around Athens, listening to the music of Stone's hounds.

The main contemporaneous source of information we are left with that helps give a picture of what foxhunting with Iroquois might have been like at this time is Williams's own book, *Horse and Hound*, which was published in 1905. In it, he lays out his hunting philosophy, including his views on everything from women participating in the chase to the best method of kenneling hounds and the most useful type of hunting horn a person could carry.

In *Horse and Hound*, Williams also gives his opinion on the best type of hound to be used, and his verdict was unequivocal—American hounds could not be bettered:

> *Hunting in America requires an altogether different hound from England, conditions being very dissimilar. Here hounds require superior hunting ability, wide ranging, greater perseverance and patience, and, above all, a much better nose to enable them to take an old and cold track, probably made the day before, and work it out inch by inch for six or eight hours if necessary. If there are any such hounds in England, they have never been sent to this country.*

On the face of it, this might seem an odd choice. American hounds had, in large part, been bred for night hunting, and their breeders had aimed at producing animals with high levels of independence—not the best qualities for pack hunting during the day.

But General Williams was a man in tune with his time. In the years preceding his book's publication, a fierce debate had raged among foxhunters about the virtues of American and English hounds for use in English-style hunting. The year 1905 proved to be the pivotal one—not just in that debate but also in the history of foxhunting in America. It marked the point at which Virginia became the *de facto* headquarters of the sport—at least as far as the northern metropolitan elite was concerned—in the same way that Leicestershire was for the English. And the events that unfolded that year also led directly to the creation of the Masters of Foxhounds Association, the organization that would oversee hunting in America for the next one hundred years. The incident that sparked these changes was known as the

Great Hound Match, and for the first time, it pitted American hounds and English hounds against one another in an effort to determine, once and for all, which was best at hunting the red fox in America. At stake were reputation and $2,000 of prize money.

THE GREAT HOUND MATCH

The match started with two gentlemen from Massachusetts, bitter enemies and each equally certain of the merits of his own hounds, whose salient characteristics they themselves often uncannily echoed. On the American side stood Harry Worcester Smith, founder and Master of the Grafton Hunt and, since 1904, also Master of the Piedmont Hunt in Virginia. A self-made millionaire, Worcester Smith was fiercely competitive, brash and, like his hounds, prone to be rather outspoken. He was also extremely confident. When he took the Mastership of the Westmeath Hunt in Ireland in 1912, Worcester Smith's "entourage included sixteen Thoroughbred horses, a pack of American hounds, five African-American grooms, a yellow open-top sports car, a yellow sulky, and three fighting cocks."[33] In 1904, he laid the seeds of the Great Hound Match by writing in the *Rider and Driver*, "Shall we hold to the heavy English type or shall we go to the racing type, that type which is the successful hound to kill a fox and acknowledged by and proven so by our own trials?"

On the English side stood Alexander Henry Higginson, known everywhere as Henry. Higginson was not suited to a life in business, a fact his father recognized as soon as his son left Harvard. Instead, Major Higginson bought Henry a farm, equipped him with a stable full of horses and a kennel full of foxhounds and watched admiringly as his son created one of the most respected hunts in America, the Middlesex. Like many other foxhunting proponents of English hounds, Higginson vehemently disagreed with Worcester Smith's opinions. Higginson's riposte, however, which was also printed in the *Rider and Driver*, went one step further:

> *Let Mr. Smith choose a judge, let me choose a judge, let the two name a third. Then let Mr. Smith go to any fair foxhunting country in America with such hounds as he chooses—and I will bring such clean-bred hounds as I choose*

> *and my huntsman and whippers-in—and we'll hunt on alternate days for love, money, or marbles. Then if his hounds kill more foxes than mine or show better sport, I'll admit I'm wrong—but not till then.*

It was a challenge Worcester Smith lost no time in accepting.

The chief bone of contention was that on the one hand, English hounds—bigger and heavier than their American cousins—were too slow to catch fast-running American foxes, while the American hounds, bred originally for independence, were too "unbiddable" to hunt as a pack. But beneath it was the obvious rivalry between the world's great superpower and the nation that would, as was becoming increasingly obvious, soon overtake it. As was only to be expected, the match caught the attention of the nation.

In the months it took to agree to terms and fix a date, the invective flying between the two camps became increasingly acrimonious. And Smith, for his part, made it clear that at stake was American pride, not just the ability of the country's hounds.

Eventually, everything was arranged—the match was to take place in November in the Piedmont Valley of Virginia. The two Masters were each to nominate one judge, and a third would be appointed by them both. True to their respective natures, the two Masters approached the contest in markedly differing styles. Higginson contented himself with ordering a completely new pack of hounds (twenty of the twenty-five couple he would eventually take to Virginia) from the Fernie in England and calmly awaited their arrival. He filled the remaining time in his usual way by hunting with the Middlesex. Worcester Smith, by contrast, went to work. Determined to leave no stone unturned in his quest to ensure his hounds' success, he almost invalidated the result before the contest could start. The rules of the match stipulated that the two packs were to have no prior hunting in the country being used for the contest. Higginson was not concerned. The natural biddability of his English hounds would allow him to control them in unfamiliar country with little difficulty. But the rule potentially put Worcester Smith's American hounds at a serious disadvantage. Their independence would make it hard to ensure they didn't all simply disappear as soon as they were unboxed on the first day, rendering the contest moot due to a lack of American hounds with which to hunt. Worcester Smith tested the rule to the limit. Taking care not to actually hunt, he took his small pack (small in order to offset the problems of control) of Virginia- and Kentucky-bred hounds to the Middleburg area in the month before the match and walked them over every inch of the country. In this way, he hoped to ensure every hound knew how to get back to the kennel should it find itself alone.

The match began on November 1. Higginson's Middlesex pack was first to hunt. The English hounds had arrived a few days before, and at seven o'clock, they were ready to start. But Higginson did not get to the meet until an hour later, seriously impairing his pack's chances of finding a fox. They drew a blank, and Higginson made sure never to be late again. The next day was the turn of the Grafton, but they, too, drew a blank. So far, the results were disappointing for both sides, but honors were even. On the third day, the Middlesex struck gold. In scenting conditions described as "only fair," the English hounds found a fox and ran it for forty-seven minutes without a check, "even giving tongue as they swam across a creek." From then on, the contest ran neck and neck.

On day four, the Grafton pack ran a fox for one and a half hours, "losing all but nine of the 28-horse field in their sizzling pace." On the fifth day, the English hounds had perhaps their finest moment, starting a red fox in Bald Hill woods and driving him hard for nearly an hour before denning him in the Goose Creek bottoms. "As he entered the covert the hounds were running on sight. [E]very one of the 37 hounds were up; the first flight will bear witness that a blanket could have covered the lot as they pressed into the woods which sheltered the quarry's refuge."

It seemed as though Higginson's hounds were beginning to change opinions. As one judge, James K. Maddux, reportedly said, "the day had proved a revelation to him as he had no idea English hounds could run so fast and true in the stiff country of the Piedmont valley."

Meanwhile, the match held the nation in its spell. Readers in New York, Washington and Boston were all kept abreast of the latest news on a daily basis. Hounds taking part in the match became as familiar as leading sports stars. As the *Boston Evening Transcript* reported on November 14: "Harry W. Smith took his six couples of American foxhounds to the meet, eleven miles from Oakley, in a hunting wagon. He hunted today the same pack of twelve hounds that has represented the Grafton the last few hunting days, with Sue and Sinbad running in place of Speckle and Sligo."

On Sunday, November 5, at the midpoint of the match and as the two packs took a rest, foxhunters and sporting people across the nation flooded into Upperville and Warrenton, intent on witnessing what the following week would bring. They saw some wonderful sport, but those hoping for a decisive victory for one side or the other were to be disappointed.

The first few days produced mixed results, with the Middlesex hounds being criticized for lack of speed and the Grafton struggling to find anything.

When they did, they soon lost the scent, and on two occasions the judge nominated by Worcester Smith intervened to help them find again. Honors continued to be even.

And so the final day's hunting for the English hounds dawned. It was to be a sad finale. Within minutes of moving off from the meet, as the hounds and huntsman turned off the road and into a field on the way to the first covert, a red fox ran straight into them. It stood no chance and was dead within minutes. On the face of it, Henry Higginson's English hounds had accounted for the first kill of the match, but he, like everyone else, was suspicious. They were right to be. At Higginson's request, an inquiry was held and it revealed that,"a man named Hall had bought a fox for $4.50 the day before and then, Hall said, the fox had escaped from him in the vicinity of the covert." The kill was discounted. The American hounds of the Grafton Hunt would have one chance to take the prize on the following day.

Saturday, November 12, was cold and clear with good scenting conditions, and the Grafton pack was soon into its stride. "The pack quickly got up one fox, then another, and split with two couple running the first and four couple running the second."[31] Although a split in the pack is never desirable, the Grafton made amends, as one of the judges reported, "I went as fast as I could gallop to Steptoe Hill…when I got there I found the entire pack giving beautiful music. Three foxes broke away in different directions, the pack took up one line, [and] stuck to it. The run was fast and notwithstanding the cold weather, the hounds held to the line and their tongue each." But at 10:15 a.m., the Grafton hounds lost their fox. Unable to find it again, the Great Hound Match of 1905 came to what many considered to be an inconclusive end.

All that remained was for the judges to give their verdict. When it came, it was a single, definitive line: "We award the Match and the stake together with the Townsend Cup to the Grafton Hounds, they, in our opinion, having done the best work with the object of killing the fox in view."

Even among the editors of the *Rider and Driver*, the paper in whose pages the challenge had been made and accepted, there was bemusement: "As may be noted by the account elsewhere the English hounds were no doubt working under some serious handicaps. On two occasions the American hounds were lifted by judges and laid on the line of scent. These incidents were not permitted to weigh with the judges in reaching their decision."

Henry Higginson accepted the decision gracefully, while Harry Worcester Smith "took the win as a complete vindication of his view that the American hound was the best animal for hunting the red fox in America." His jubilation was not to last. Within a year of the match, Worcester Smith had resigned the Mastership of the Piedmont, sold his hounds and left Virginia, in part because foxhunters drawn to the area by the contest openly disregarded the etiquette of hunting and made repeated incursions into the Piedmont's county. In vain, Worcester Smith appealed to the ineffectual National Steeplechase and Hunt Association, which aimed to oversee the sport, and to which General Williams and the Iroquois Hunt belonged. Worcester Smith was determined that no other Master and hunt should be placed in a similar position, and together with five others, he founded the Masters of Foxhounds Association of America on February 14, 1907.

The Great Hound Match of 1905 might well have been considered merely a dispute between two northerners for whom the ability of hounds to kill, rather than chase, foxes was all important. New England foxhunters had a reputation for taking a much more aggressive approach, as John Fox explained:

> *The man from the Brunswick Fur Club* [in Maine] *explained that in his country the sportsmen shot the foxes because the hounds could not catch them fast enough. The foxes were so thick up there that people could hardly raise a Thanksgiving turkey. So they shot them to appease the farmers, whom they had to fight annually in the Legislature to prevent them having the fox exterminated by law as a pest.*

That attitude contrasted markedly with the one that prevailed farther south. As Fox commented, "Provided he has had the fun of the chase, the Kentucky hunter is secretly glad, I believe, that the little fellow has gone scot-free." Nevertheless, Kentuckians and Virginians were intensely interested in the match for the obvious reason that it pitted their hounds against those from elsewhere.

Williams, however, was much more than simply an interested observer. His support for the American hound might have found its most definite and lasting expression in the pages of his book, *Horse and Hound*. But for many years prior to 1905, Williams had been trying to establish a recognized breed type for the American hound similar to that enjoyed by the English foxhound. Through the auspices of the National Foxhunters Association, he had introduced the American Foxhound Stud Book in 1892 to encourage keeping records of all pedigrees. At the same time, he also introduced bench shows to Kentucky to look at the conformation of hounds in an effort to encourage an improved standard. This initiative, like his desire to found an organized hunt club, was initially greeted with a certain amount of skepticism by his fellow foxhunters but soon enthusiastically taken up.

Ironically, given the criticism that would be leveled at Williams's Iroquois Hunt in the 1920s by people who believed it to have been an informal and disorganized affair, Williams's ultimate goal was organization because that was where he felt English hunting's greatest strength lay. As the Thoroughbred breeders of Williams's native state also found, honest and accurate record keeping provided the key to improving the breed.

The development of field trials and bench shows, and the debate over the relative superiority of American over English hounds that culminated in 1905, also became central to the story of the Iroquois Hunt because Williams's opinions exerted an enormous influence over the sportsmen and women who would succeed him. Although English huntsmen would be employed and, occasionally, English hounds tried, in the end, every succeeding generation at Iroquois, up to the 1990s, followed his lead in their preference for American hounds—and in particular the strain developed by Williams's great friends, the Walker family of Garrard County. As Charlotte Pursley said in 2002, "We had good Kentucky hounds. We didn't want English hounds."[35]

The result of the Great Hound Match might be seen as vindication for the supporters of the American foxhound, of which Roger Williams was a leading member. It certainly confirmed Williams's view, and as a result, it had a lasting impact on the Iroquois Hunt over the next ninety years. Today, the Iroquois Hunt Club is famous across the nation for the quality of its English hounds. But the story of how the hunt arrived at such a complete *volte-face* will have to wait until the final chapter and the arrival of a new type of quarry and a new kind of Master.

Ours Is Not to Reason Why...

Given his determined support for the American-bred hound, it seems reasonable to ask why Roger Williams should have wanted to establish an English-style hunt in Kentucky in the first place, particularly considering the opposition he encountered. In fact, did he even set out to establish such a hunt or was that the retrospective assumption of a younger generation of sportsmen? On balance, it seems probable that he did and that the officers of the club, at least, dressed the part, as John Fox's reference to "bang tail horses and top boots" suggests. Williams's views reflect the general ambivalence many Americans felt toward the English at that time. Undoubtedly, there were things he admired about English hunting—his efforts to create a breed standard and studbook for American hounds show how much he valued their method. Just as important, however, was the opportunity English hunting provided for socializing and entertaining, for healthy exercise and, first and foremost for a man obsessed with hounds and hunting, for seeing more of the hound work he adored.

Nevertheless, the Iroquois Hunt was extremely "democratic" in what its members—and its leader—chose to hunt. Rabbits, wolves and foxes were all pursued and were often specially imported for the chase. And although Williams said in *Horse and Hound*, "I care more for one good daylight run than a month of night hunting," in the 1890s and 1900s—if the evidence of the newspapers is to be believed—Iroquois was to be found night hunting and field trialing at least as often as it was to be seen following hounds in the English style

Over the next twenty-four years, from 1890 to 1914, the Iroquois Hunting and Riding Club took part in many events. Race meetings, parties, polo matches, dances and rabbit, raccoon and, presumably, fox hunts all continued to take place. Then, in 1914, General Williams was called away on military duty, eventually being placed in command of a section of border between the United States and Mexico as war threatened between the two countries in 1916, then ending up in France following America's entry into the First World War. In his absence, his daughter Mary tried to keep the club alive. But the dwindling supplies of horses, grooms and workers able to keep the bridle paths open made the task impossible, and from 1914 on, there are no more records in the Lexington press of the happenings at the Iroquois Hunt.

Chapter 3

Revival

The End of the Beginning

The fall of 1925 brought sad news and, apparently, an irrevocable end to any chance of re-founding the old Iroquois Hunting and Riding Club. On Saturday, December 12, at 1:40 p.m., General Roger D. Williams died. He was sixty-nine. Seemingly in excellent health, he had spent the previous evening at the theater,[36] indulging in one of his life's most consistent sources of enjoyment. He awoke at his home at 217 South Ashland Avenue in Lexington the next morning complaining of chest pains and was too ill to leave his bed. Doctors were summoned, but before any treatment could be given, the General died of a massive heart attack. The afternoon editions of the Lexington papers carried front-page obituaries. And over the next week, tributes poured in from around the country. Presidents, diplomats, army officers and hunters all wrote of their sadness at his loss and of the immense contribution he had made to life in Kentucky and the nation. His fellow Kentuckian and officer Major General Henry Allen[37] wrote, "The passing of one of Kentucky's historic figures and one of the nation's most worthy patriots has left a vacancy that cannot easily be filled. Individuals possessed of such virility and magnetism are born at rare intervals."

On Tuesday, December 15, after a brief service at St. Peter's Catholic Church conducted by Father C.A. Towell, General Williams was laid to rest in the family plot at Lexington Cemetery. As the *Lexington Herald* wrote,

"Simplicity and dignity will mark the services. A military farewell to the brilliant solder will be paid as 'Taps' is sounded by a bugler." Among the pallbearers were his friends and hunting companions Desha Breckinridge, C.H. Berryman, J.E. Bassett and Joseph Le Comte.

Almost two weeks later, on Christmas Eve, the General's widow received a telegram addressed to him from the French government. It contained the posthumous award of the Legion D'Honneur for his service during the First World War. The honor had been arranged by the French military attaché in Washington, Major Georges Thenault,[38] who had not heard of the General's death. It read, "Great pleasure to announce you have been appointed officer Legion of Honor. Congratulations."

General Williams's interest in hunting had never wavered. After his return from France in 1920, he continued to attend and judge field trials and bench shows and remained active in the National Foxhunters Association and the Masters of Foxhounds Association, serving as vice-president of the MFHA in 1908. Rookwood Kennels and Bonnie Stone continued to sell successful hunting hounds all over the country. But there is no evidence to suggest that Williams ever thought seriously about reforming the Iroquois Hunt. Perhaps he felt such an active role should be taken up by a younger generation. If so, there was no shortage of candidates or enthusiasm.

The first attempt came in 1923, when the officers of the Lexington Cavalry Club tried to establish a hunt. Busily recruiting members and looking out for suitable hounds, Captains Cabel Breckinridge and Frank Wright of C Troop wrote to one prospective member (Frances Lathrop Smith) in September that "we have every reason to believe that we will have within the next week sufficient money to buy a pack of hounds and employ a huntsman." The aim was to hunt twice a week at Crab Orchard, but an inability to raise sufficient funds meant that the effort came to nothing.[39]

At the same time, there were also many civilians agitating to restart the town's sporting activity throughout the early 1920s.

Finally, on the evening of November 6, 1926, barely eleven months after the General's death, fourteen of these local sportsmen hosted a dinner at Colonel E.R. Bradley's newly established Ashland Country Club—forerunner of the Idle Hour Country Club—and there it was decided to reform the General's most significant creation, at least as far as the citizens of Lexington were concerned, the Iroquois Hunt.

It is tempting to think of the re-founding of the Iroquois Hunt Club as having taken place spontaneously after a convivial evening and a good dinner, perhaps as the guests were reminiscing about General Williams and the stories their parents had told them of hunting with him before the First World War, but the meeting at the Ashland Club in November 1926 was carefully planned. Several people were invited to address the assembled company during dinner, including W.V. Thraves of the Deep Run Hunt near Richmond, Virginia, and Elliott S. Nichols, MFH, of the Bloomfield Open Hunt near Detroit. At the end of their speeches, a vote was taken, and the Iroquois Hunt was officially reborn. Officers were quickly appointed, with William Preston being elected president, Len Shouse and Kendall McDowell joint-Masters of Foxhounds and Churchill Newcomb secretary. Mary Sayre Combs, General Williams's daughter, was made honorary president.

In fact, while the records of the first incarnation of the Iroquois Hunt revolve entirely around the leadership of General Williams, in its second and more permanent incarnation, the club had almost an overabundance of leaders, at least in its first few years. The president, William Preston—six feet, six inches tall and weighing close to 250 pounds—was a descendant of one of Lexington's most prominent families; the club's secretary, John Churchill Newcomb, was a former editor of the *Harvard Lampoon* and presided over *The Chase* magazine; and Len Shouse, one of the first Masters, was the owner of Lexington's most luxurious hotel, the Lafayette. Others included Arnold Hanger, whose family firm built the Grand Coulee Dam and much of New York's subway; Kendall McDowell, grandson-in-law of one of America's richest men; Major Louie Beard, former international polo player and manager of one of Lexington's most prestigious Thoroughbred farms; and John Gourlay, a native of Melrose, Scotland, who managed a subsidiary of the Superior Oil Company. All of these people played significant roles in helping establish the club on a sound footing. All were strong personalities, successful, intelligent and, to a greater or lesser degree, obsessed with hounds and hunting. From the start, however, there was a division of interest. The younger members—Newcomb, Gourlay and Hanger—aimed at establishing an English-style hunt while Shouse, Preston and Combs preferred field trials.

As a first principle, all the members agreed that the new club needed to be built on more solid and permanent foundations if it was to survive the vicissitudes of changing personnel that had so hampered the original hunt. As John Gourlay, a future Iroquois secretary, wrote in *The Chase* magazine in February 1927, the new club was founded by people "who are not treading on entirely unfamiliar ground, who have looked into the matter with care and forethought, who are willing to go ahead slowly on small beginnings, whose interest was not born overnight and whose efforts will not cease on the morrow."

In accordance with this cautious approach, the first decision taken by the members at the Ashland Club dinner was to see how much demand there really was for the new hunt with local sportsmen. To test the water, they arranged a paper chase for the following day in the grounds of Ashland, the former home of Henry Clay and just next door to the Ashland Club. As Gourlay's 1927 article in *The Chase* continued, "The next day, 23 members met in the oak-studded meadows of Ashland to take part in a paper chase." Clearly, "23 members" was enough for the organizers to decide to move forward with their plans. "A few weeks later, on Thanksgiving Day, the first drag hunt was held on the old Norwood place."[40]

A photograph depicting the new club's first paper chase at Ashland still exists. It shows a group of happy riders, dressed in everyday riding clothes of the period, basking in the sunshine and enjoying the beautiful scenery of Ashland's grounds. To them, it couldn't have seemed that different from many of their usual rides.

The first hunt, however, was a very different affair. Charles Kendall McDowell, one of the two joint-Masters appointed earlier that month, wrote to prospective participants to explain the proceedings: "A splendid drag course has been laid over five or six farms so that you may look forward to a run of about six miles…over blue grass pastures and other smooth galloping land. After the drag if the members desire a rabbit hunt, they may return to the estate of Dr. Halley, who has very generously given permission to hold one on his land." After some detailed advice about where to obtain a mount if members did not have one of their own readily available, he concluded, "You will be interested to know that ten couples of foxhounds have been purchased and are now being worked near Lexington. Necessarily the pack is at present very much of a scratch affair and the meet will be most informal, but you will not be disappointed if you enjoy a good ride behind hounds." First, though, members would gather for breakfast at the Chimney Corners Tea Room at 8:30 a.m.

Thanksgiving Day 1926—The First Hunt

Held at 9:30 a.m. on Thanksgiving Day, November 25, 1926, the first hunt took place at a group of farms north of the town and bordered on the west by Leestown Pike and on the east by Georgetown Road. Twenty hounds were collected and trained by Bonnie Stone, still living near the old Rookwood

Kennels on Athens-Boonesboro Road and still an active night hunter at age fifty-four. Hounds and riders met at the gates of Meadowthorpe Farm just before 9:30 a.m., and hounds moved off promptly.

While the breakfast that preceded it at the Chimney Corners Tea Room "represented in every particular a hunt breakfast of days gone by and which in some respects resembled a hunt dinner," the hunt itself proved tougher going, and the elements conspired to do their worst to test the commitment of the new club's first participants. As *The Chase* magazine reflected in February 1927:

> *Meanwhile, the heavens opened and there was a Kentucky rain which would have kept less enthusiastic sportsmen and sportswomen from taking the saddle. How it did pour! Yet every one of the forty-eight members who put in an appearance and a few others who came later climbed into the saddle and enjoyed a run across the blue grass pastures, through the deep furrowed road of a wheat field, across streams and up hills to a finish six miles away with not one check.*

Rain was not the only problem. Many of the participants were not even sure what was happening during the ride. As Charlotte Pursley recalled many years later, "I kept to the side and then I saw people waving me on, so I rode on a bit more, and then they said, 'You've won!'" But it was enough; people were hooked. Concluding its 1927 summary, *The Chase* magazine recorded, "Since that time there have been drags every Saturday that the weather permitted and never have there been less than twenty persons out, despite the worst imaginable conditions of frost and cold that a winter may provide." The new hunt was up and running, and under the careful guidance of the president, Masters and secretary it grew rapidly over the course of the next two years.

A Huntsman Named Hall

Throughout the winter of 1926–27, Iroquois continued to hold drag hunts on locations north of the town, mostly on farms near the Leestown and Newtown Pikes. The intention was to establish a proper hunt, but only when enough time had elapsed to purchase and train hounds and to find a permanent "country" in which to operate. An early opportunity for some new country presented itself in January 1927.

On January 11, just two months after the first hunt, the two Masters (Shouse and Kendall McDowell) were able to write to members and friends, "We have been invited by the landowners and farmers in the neighborhood of Athens to hunt in their country. We met there last Saturday for a drag hunt…courtesy of Mr. Morgan Gentry, and I do not believe a more beautiful hunting country exists, than that which lay before us."

The land they had been invited to hunt across was the old stomping ground of General Williams and still home to Bonnie Stone. The village stood on a ridge about three quarters of a mile long and half a mile wide. To the north was open farmland, consisting of wooded coverts and gently undulating hills, while to the south and east the land formed part of the watershed of Boone Creek, named by those eponymously obsessed early settlers not for Daniel Boone but his brother Edward, who was killed there in 1780. The waters of several smaller creeks—Baughman Fork, Boggs Fork and Jones Creek—fed into Boone Creek before it emptied into the Kentucky. Farther east, another watershed, Jouett Creek, also drained into the Kentucky River. The creeks had cut deep channels into the easily dissolvable limestone that lay under the whole region.

The hunt referred to in the Masters' letter of January 11, 1927, marked a move away from drag hunting and toward the pursuit of live quarry. But it was still a hunt with a difference, as the pack was to consist of an assortment of hounds collected on the day of the meet. "On Saturday, January 15th at 10 o'clock…the Iroquois Hunt will sponsor a fox hunt for its members and the people living in the Athens neighborhood," wrote Kendall McDowell. "Hounds will meet at Bonnie Stone's on the Athens-Boonesboro Pike. Let's all make our plans now and be on hand to have a good old fashioned fox hunt. All owners of hounds in the neighborhood are invited to bring not more than two couples for the chase. Bonnie Stone will act as Huntsman and L.B. Shouse will be Master of Hounds. It is requested that everyone that can do so come mounted." Provision was made for bad weather, in which case the hunt would either be postponed or a drag substituted. It is clear that until this point the Iroquois pack was a drag pack only, and perhaps it was for this reason that members of the Athens community were invited to bring their own hounds. As usual, the hunt was preceded by a hunt breakfast at the Chimney Corners Tea Room.

In order to take things forward, what was needed was a professional huntsman who could mold the hounds into a pack, help show members good sport and instruct Masters and members alike—many of them being confirmed field trialers—in the art of English foxhunting. The man Iroquois found was Captain Walter Hall, a nephew of the Master of the Border Hunt in England.

Recruited in August 1927 for the coming season (1927–28), Walter Hall was an Englishman who had immigrated to Canada and then ended up as huntsman to Mr. Marland's Hounds, the property of oil millionaire E.W. Marland[41] in Ponca City, Oklahoma. Marland was head of what later became Conoco Oil, and in the course of his often controversial life, he made and lost several fortunes. The 1920s saw him flush with success and determined to introduce foxhunting and polo to Oklahoma's smart set. To do so, he also had to introduce the red fox to the state. Marland, Hall and the Master of Foxhounds, Major Donald Henderson—a former British cavalry officer—set about hunting not only foxes but also hares, rabbits and wolves. They also helped the nearby Artillery Hunt with drafts of hounds.

There were several points of contact between Mr. Marland's Hounds and the Iroquois Hunt. Churchill Newcomb had reported on the hunting in Oklahoma for *The Chase*, and Arnold Hanger had hunted there, too. John Gourlay, their mutual friend, knew Marland through his connection to the oil industry, and both Gourlay and another Iroquois member, Sam Wooldridge, had seen Hall hunt Marland's hounds. It is likely, though not certain, that Gourlay, Hanger and Newcomb were the ones who recruited Hall to come to Kentucky because they were the members who were most enthusiastic about riding to hounds in the English manner.

In the fall of 1927, Walter Hall packed up his belongings in Oklahoma and made the long journey to Lexington, Kentucky. The hunt he had joined might have been new, but it was growing rapidly. In 1927, the hunt had forty-eight members, but by early 1928, the number had risen to seventy-two. And for the 1927–28 season, Iroquois planned to have two separate packs, one to hunt fox and one for drag hunting.[42] The local farmers and horse breeders were, by now, more sanguine about the hunt crossing their land, even with a pack of hounds. The hounds Hall would need to train were kenneled with Bonnie Stone on Walnut Hill Road just outside Athens, and the records show that they were all American of the Walker type.

Hunting, however, was not the only concern of the people in charge of the club. They were determined to build from the ground up the kind of hunt that forms a linchpin of the local community. Throughout 1928, the club's extramural activities increased and gathered pace. That same year saw the introduction of the first Horse and Hound Show, the first Iroquois field trial and the first farmers' dinner. Sadly, it also saw the departure of the club secretary, Churchill Newcomb, who left to take up the post of editor of the *American Field*. Newcomb's successor as the Iroquois secretary was John Gourlay.

J. Churchill Newcomb

In several important ways, Churchill Newcomb could lay claim to being the man most responsible for the Iroquois Hunt Club as it came to develop over the succeeding decades. A resident of Kentucky, Virginia and New York, on his father's side, Churchill Newcomb was a descendant of Colonel Andrew Newcomb, who lived in Boston in 1640. More recently, the Newcomb family had been responsible for the Louisville & Nashville Railroad, of which Newcomb's grandfather and great-grandfather had been presidents. They had also organized and run the United States National Bank in New York. His mother's family, the Churchills, had given Louisville its first racetrack in 1830, and in 1874, they gave it another. The land they ceded for this second track became known as Churchill Downs, home of the Kentucky Derby. Of middle height, with blue eyes and fine, sandy-colored hair, Newcomb was a cultured individual, a patron of the arts and collector of rare books who was himself a fine writer. His first wife, Margaret, was the daughter of George Julian Zolnay, known as the "sculptor of the Confederacy" and today regarded as one of the finest artists of the early twentieth century. After graduating from Harvard in 1923, where he was editor of the *Harvard Lampoon*, Newcomb came to Lexington to manage and edit *The Chase* magazine, the official organ of American foxhunting. It was an ideal position from which to pursue the two presiding passions of his life: hunting and writing.

The evidence that Newcomb's was the hand guiding Iroquois in 1926 and 1927 comes from a letter written to Henry Vaughan, the urbane secretary—and future president—of the Masters of Foxhounds Association and a fellow graduate of Harvard, who conducted all the nation's hunting business from his law office in Boston. On November 16, 1926, two weeks into the life of the new club, Newcomb wrote to Vaughan:

> *Needless to say…I am having all manner of difficulties in trying to introduce a practically new form of an old game in Central Kentucky. I*

> *was able to write the Constitution and By-laws and dictate the officers for the first year, and I am glad to report we have a very alert young man as one of the joint masters. But, I feel that we must begin at the very bottom and begin slowly, working up finally to a crack Hunt. The danger is that it will get out of hand and degenerate into an informal sporting outfit, such as the old Iroquois. The fight down here is not to get people out for sport, but to make them play the game according to Hoyle.*[43] *Independence of action has its drawbacks as well as benefits.*

Newcomb was well acquainted with the old Iroquois Hunt. His parents had hunted often with General Williams and Solomon Van Meter at Shenandoah Hall. But while the letter quoted above could give the impression that Newcomb had a snobbish preference for English hunting, in fact, the contrary is true—he was a passionate advocate of all breeds of hounds and all types of hunting. Nonetheless, he and the younger members of the new club—principally Beard, Gourlay and Hanger—were the ones who were most enthusiastic about English-style hunting.

Although Newcomb did not stay long in Lexington, he continued to keep an eye on life at the Iroquois Hunt. And through him we have a detailed record of the club's inaugural Horse and Hound Show, held at the H.P. Whitney farm on May 10, 1928, which Newcomb reported in the pages of another newspaper to which he made occasional contributions, the *Wall Street Journal*.

Organized with consummate skill by Harry Payne Whitney's farm manager and Iroquois member Major Louie Beard, the inaugural Iroquois Hunt Horse and Hound Show attracted an audience of over 1,200 people and, helped by the one-dollar charge for admittance, put the club's finances on sound footing for the year. Attendees could also purchase a beautifully produced souvenir program, decorated with a black cover bisected by a wide diagonal stripe of palest Iroquois blue and a medallion in the center depicting the head of Iroquois, the horse for whom the original hunt had been named. (A year later, the program also included a map of the hunt country revealing the location of all the illicit stills. Though whether this was a warning or a guide for thirsty Prohibition-era foxhunters is not known. Nor is it clear quite how the mapmakers knew of the locations in the first place.) The morning and early part of the afternoon were devoted to a horse show involving not just hunter and jumping classes for both adults and children but also opportunities for the owners of three- and five-gaited horses and even an "Open Mule Race, course to be laid over one mile of open country, first prize a silver trophy donated by Halley and Preston," in which "the colors of Miss Elizabeth Daingerfield, breeder, writer, and guardian of Man o' War, went down to defeat before Berry Clark on Midget."

As well as a silver trophy for the winner, donated either by a local business or an individual, the first, second and third in each class were also given a blue, red or yellow ribbon. Lunch was served from 12:30 p.m. until 2:00 p.m., after which the horse show continued with classes for green hunters, three-gaited saddle horses and ladies' hunters. The show concluded with a ladies' and gentlemen's jumping class.

The hound show held the same day had six classes, including "Best Pack Owned by a Hunt Club," and hounds from nearby hunts in Cincinnati (Camargo), Louisville (Muldraugh)[44] and Virginia (Rappahannock) took part. Writing in the *Wall Street Journal*, Newcomb described the show as "the first private hunt show in the history of Central Kentucky." And apart from the beauty of the setting, what impressed him most was the speed with which the hunt had taken hold in the community. As he wrote, "The extraordinary thing is that the hunting and jumping fever only returned to Lexington about 18 months ago." The members were all to be congratulated on getting their mounts ready for the event over the space of a few weeks, many not having expected to enter at all. "Albert Kane entered the novice class on a seven-year-old brood mare, Hestia, belonging to Mr. Miller of New York, who now rents the old Belmont Nursery, and actually got to the third fence with only two weeks of schooling behind his mount," Newcomb wrote. "J.E. Kittrell was equally determined to win with his 17-year-old Nip II which, he explained, had won several hundred thousand on the flat and was going to make a hunter yet." Chief among those to be credited with this transformation was the Iroquois huntsman, Captain Walter Hall, who "insists on a horse coming into its jumps well collected…he rides as a gentleman should."

But the star turn of the first show was not a gentleman but a lady and one who would, in time, become central to the life of the club. "Easily the best exhibition of the day was the riding of Miss Charlotte Bowman [the future Charlotte Pursley] with form equally faultless on a saddle horse or a hunter," said Newcomb.

The club's events for 1928 did not end with the Horse and Hound Show. In October, the first Annual Farmers Dinner and Foxhunt was held at 6:30 p.m. at Grimes Mill. From the start, the Masters and officers emphasized the importance of maintaining good relations with the owners of the land. And in December, there was a field trial, put on for the farmers as much as for the members. All local sportsmen who had hounds were invited to take part, and their animals could be registered with Bonnie Stone and Captain Hall, who would be responsible for painting on numbers and organizing the event.

A month later, on November 3, the club celebrated its first St. Hubert's Day in honor of the patron saint of hunting with a hunt starting at 7:00 a.m., also from Grimes Mill. Members were treated to a poem written for the occasion by Len Shouse and placed on the bottom of the invitation:

St. Hubert was a sporty gent
Before he joined the church
Now he is our patron saint
If that will help us much.

The hunt's fixture cards and invitations from this period often contained poetry from Shouse's pen and were invariably decorated with hunting scenes by Gourlay.

The last non-hunting activity of the year occurred in November, when the club held its first annual meeting. Gourlay's report, a copy of which was sent to the Masters of Foxhounds Association, summarizes the achievements as they saw them:

> *Two years ago we started with a lot of enthusiasm, a big debt, some very mediocre horses, and a few cull hounds. The only saving thing we had was the best hunting country in America owned by the best sporting farmers to be found anywhere. Tonight we still have the enthusiasm and a few of the debts, but our members now own horses that are hard to beat in any hunting country, our pack is improved, and our hunting country is opened up for mile after mile. We now own ten of the most picturesque acres in Central Kentucky, an historic building, which is our headquarters, commodious stables in town and on the hunting country property, excellent kennels, and an increasing membership.*

Gourlay continued by recalling the visits to Iroquois made during the past season by two of "the greatest living authorities on Foxhunting. Men who are familiar with hunting in Scotland, England, Ireland, France, Germany, Belgium, and Spain."

Joseph B. Thomas and Harry Worcester Smith had both visited Iroquois during 1928. Thomas had endeared himself to the members by "being loud in his praise" of the hunting country but then ruined the effect by adding that it needed only "about sixty thousand dollars spent on it to panel[15] it, while a paltry ten thousand would be required for a kennel." In fact, as Gourlay noted, the kennel had been completed that year at a cost of $300, and joint-Master Arnold Hanger was paneling the country for considerably less than $60,000. Worcester Smith wisely confined himself to compliments and was "so apparently sincere" that the club's directors made him an honorary member of the hunt for life. Thomas was not accorded a similar honor.

The club had also played host to Elliott Nichols of the Bloomington Open Hunt of Detroit, who had spoken to the fourteen sportsmen at the Ashland Club back in October 1926. Nichols brought his hounds with him en route home from Nashville, and the Bloomington pack spent two happy days hunting the Iroquois country.

The visits were not simply social calls. Although anxious to encourage the growth of the sport across America, the Masters of Foxhounds Association was nonetheless careful in deciding which hunts to recognize formally. At least two years had to elapse from the time a club was founded until it was accepted into the fold because so many had been started with the best of intentions, only to fail as soon as the initial enthusiasm waned. Unofficial inspections, such as the visits paid by Thomas and Worcester Smith, satisfied the hierarchy that clubs had been set upon a sound footing and were likely to prosper.

Gourlay singled out three individuals for their exceptional contribution to the life of the hunt: Len Shouse, to whose lot "the hard problem of furnishing sport" had fallen and who had evidently accomplished his allotted task with great success; Captain Armstrong, head of the "ladies' riding party [which] can be seen on the bridle path…three days a week" and which was constantly attracting new riders ("as each new rider ultimately means a new foxhunter…the genial captain's assistance is of great value to us"; and Major Louie Beard, who received thanks for organizing "the outstanding event of the year," the Horse and Hound Show.

Gourlay's report ended in thanking the media for its help in establishing the viability of the new club—both the *Lexington Herald* and the *Kentucky Leader* had given ample coverage to the hunt's program of events, ensuring a steady increase in the applications for membership—and mourning the passing of Captain Frank Wright of the Lexington Troop, who had been instrumental in re-founding the club. His sudden death at the age of forty was a sad loss for the growing hunt.

The club began the new season of 1928–29 with two new Masters and a new huntsman. Walter Hall hunted the Iroquois hounds for just one season.

It is not known why he decided to resign; perhaps painting numbers on hounds for a field trial was the final straw. And sadly, not much is known about what happened to him after 1929. Only two further references to him can be found. One, a fleeting comment in *The Chase* magazine's account of the 1929 Horse and Hound Show—held that year at Colonel and Mrs. Haggin's Mount Brilliant Farm, already familiar in Iroquois history as the location of Russell Cave, the scene of so many parties of the old Iroquois Hunting and Riding Club—explained how Captain Hall mistakenly jumped clean out of the show ring during one class, thinking the rail was another fence. The other, from later the same day, reported a traffic accident. Hall's car had collided with an interurban tram in downtown Lexington. Neither the interurban passengers nor Hall were harmed, but Hall's passenger—a young horseman who had recently moved to Kentucky from Rappahannock County, Virginia, with his family—eventually died of his injuries. Regrettably, one other casualty that year was the mule race: 1928 was the first and last time Iroquois members have been allowed to race their mules, although Arnold Hanger's wife is said to have "hunted a spotted mule in full Corinthian attire."

Presidents, Masters and Huntsmen

The men Churchill Newcomb helped appoint to the offices of the club in 1926–28 and who guided the club over the first two years of its new life have for the most part been forgotten, eclipsed by the overwhelming personality of their predecessor General Roger D. Williams. But together with figures such as Major Louie Beard, Captain William Armstrong and John Gourlay, the first group of senior officers of the re-founded club—William Preston, Leonard Shouse and Charles Kendall McDowell—put in a huge amount of time-consuming work to ensure the club was set on the right path from its new beginning. All three might have been united by a love of hounds and hunting, but they had found their way to Iroquois from markedly different directions.

The Prestons were one of Lexington's most respected families, related to the Breckinridges, Harts and Wickcliffes. William Preston's grandfather had been the U.S. ambassador to Spain, and his great-grandfather Robert Wickliffe (known as the "Old Duke") had been Lexington's richest citizen.[46] The Preston name counted, and the new Iroquois Hunt's ties to its past and to the town were strengthened by the current William Preston's involvement.

Large and patrician, William Preston (1887–1943), known always as Squire Preston, lived on Richmond Road in Lexington and, on hunting mornings, "would drive the 12 miles to the hunt country in a break cart, with one horse pulling him and two hitched behind. Those two were for his children, Anne and Bill. The horse pulling the cart was his. When he got to the meet, he would unharness him, throw a saddle on him and away he'd go." The whole process went into reverse at the end of the day. Despite standing six feet, six inches tall and weighing close to 250 pounds, Squire Preston was a regular competitor in the Iroquois Horse Show and was frequently among the winners.

In contrast, Charles Kendall McDowell (1896–1953), known as Kendall, was not from Lexington at all. Worse still, he wasn't even from Kentucky. Born and raised in Middletown, Delaware, into a farming family with strong political connections (his younger brother Harris B. McDowell Jr. would become a long-standing Democratic Representative for the state), Kendall McDowell came to Lexington to pursue a career in farming. Once there, he met and married Alice Burt. Alice was the granddaughter of Wellington Burt, who, in the early 1900s, was considered one of the ten richest men in America. The Burt money was made from lumber, among other things, and Alice Burt's father, Charles—who was described in her wedding announcement in July 1920 as "the millionaire lumberman"—ran the company's holdings in Kentucky, which included a huge mill at Ford. Today, Ford is really little more than a telephone code and a postal address. But in 1900, over 2,500 people lived and worked in mills that ran twenty-four hours a day and seven days a week. Abandoning his plans to farm, Kendall McDowell joined the Burt family firm and became a lumberman. It wasn't all a bed of roses. The year before Kendall and Alice married, her grandfather Wellington Burt died, leaving one of the most bizarre wills in American legal history. Its "spite clause" stipulated that the inheritance could only be paid out twenty-one years after the death of Wellington Burt's last surviving grandchild. In 2010, that condition was met and the remaining money distributed. None of it made its way to Kendall and Alice, and by 1908, the mill at Ford had closed. In keeping with the close ties among hunt members, Alice's sister Lady Belle married another of the new club's most stalwart members, Clarence LeBus. Kendall McDowell was the "alert young man" mentioned in J. Churchill Newcomb's letter of November 1926.

If William Preston brought a sense of continuity and Kendall McDowell brought energy, Len Shouse brought hounds. While the other two could be said respectively to have inherited and married money and position, Len Shouse (1870–1957) earned it, living what can only be described as the archetypal American dream. Described by his grandson as "a small man with a big voice, who wasn't afraid of anything," Shouse was born on his father's farm near Taylorsville, Kentucky, in Anderson County in 1870. When he was thirteen, he and his brother were given a piece of land and allowed to farm it themselves. They spent a year growing tobacco and, when it was harvested, transported it by barge up to Louisville to sell. The profit they made was so small that for a year's work, each earned just $7.50. The next day, according to family legend, fourteen-year-old Len left the farm for good and walked the sixty miles to Lexington, taking with him his $7.50 and the clothes on his back. He had made up his mind that there was money to be made in the city. He was right. Exhausted from his journey, Len fell asleep in a field a few miles short of his destination. The owner of the field found him sleeping, but instead of chasing him off, he took him in and gave him food, clothing, a place to rest and a job on his farm. For the next few years, Len traveled about Lexington by pony and cart selling the farmer's produce. Then he started work racking pool balls at the Florentine Hotel on Main Street, where he met many of the town's sportsmen. He had found his niche. In a few years, he amassed enough capital to start a grocery business with R.T. Nugent. But from 1894 on, he ran the business with James T. Looney, who would become known to Kentuckians as the Burgoo King.[47] The grocery stood at the corner of Main and DeWees Streets, then on the very edge of the town. Shouse and Looney prospered and soon moved into the hotel business. And when they dissolved their partnership in 1908 (to allow Looney to concentrate on the grocery), Shouse was able to put together enough money to build what would quickly become one of Lexington's landmarks, the Lafayette Hotel.

Along the way, Shouse had also become obsessed with hunting, particularly night hunting and field trialing. There is no evidence that he ever hunted with the old Iroquois (at least his name never appears in any of the endless lists quoted by the local papers when covering Iroquois events), but by 1926, Len Shouse had served as president of the National Foxhunters Association and was one of the most respected hound breeders in the country. At fifty-six, he was well established in the town as a successful businessman and an immensely popular personality. "I remember he would appear in the lobby of the hotel [Lafayette] at six o'clock and welcome every person who came through the door, most of whom he knew by name," recalled his grandson Len Shouse III. Aside from Churchill Newcomb, Shouse became the prime mover in the early life of the club's second incarnation. According to Charlotte Pursley, for the first few seasons, at least, the hounds were all supplied by Shouse.

From Sperryville, Virginia

Len Shouse and Kendall McDowell's role as Masters of Iroquois ended in 1928. The men who replaced them were Arnold Hanger and William Clay McDowell. Hanger was a partner in the Mason Hanger Construction Company of Richmond, Kentucky, and New York City.[48] William McDowell managed the Phoenix Hotel and was a descendant of Henry Clay and a nephew of Nettie McDowell, the Iroquois Hunt's first vice-president in 1887. However, he was apparently not related to the man he replaced as Master, Charles Kendall McDowell.

In the absence of Captain Hall, Hanger and McDowell recruited two men from the small town of Sperryville, Virginia, to act as huntsman and whipper-in: Joseph B. Johnson and Rudolph Singleton. They were both widely experienced huntsmen, and Johnson in particular was a greatly respected hound breeder and judge. In the last few months of 1929, at what would prove to be the halfway point of his tenure at Iroquois, he was asked to be one of the four judges at the National Field Trial Championship, the ultimate accolade for anyone interested in American foxhounds and field trials.

The links between Iroquois members and the hunt country of Virginia were extremely strong in the 1920s. When Sterling Larrabee[49] was looking for a place to set up a hunt in 1923, Major Louie Beard recommended Rappahannock County as "the best country in America." Larrabee heeded Beard's advice and set up his own private hunt at Flint Hill, a pack that would eventually become known as the Old Dominion.

Described by *The Chase* magazine as "a farmer by trade," Johnson was "a splendid man over any country, a hard rider that knows hounds and how to keep up with them." In 1926, two years before he joined Iroquois, Johnson and his friend Hugh Bywaters, breeder of the famous and eponymous strain of foxhound, founded their own hunt in Sperryville. They called it the Rappahannock, after the county in which Sperryville lies. Almost ninety years later, the Rappahannock Hunt is still going strong and still one of the most respected hunts in Virginia. But for two seasons starting in 1928, while Hugh Bywaters hunted the country in Virginia, Joseph Johnson traveled to

Kentucky to act as huntsman for the Iroquois. He brought his hounds with him, and for the first time the hunt had two different strains of hound, albeit both American. From 1928 until the mid-1930s, the Iroquois pack consisted of both Walkers and Bywaters, with its most highly regarded hound of the period, Jess Hammond, being a Bywater. When Johnson returned to Virginia, his hounds went, too. But the breeding of many of Iroquois hounds in the future can be directly attributed to the Sperryville contingent's short stay in Kentucky.

Johnson's assistant, Rudolph Singleton, had other reasons to join what was still a very new club. Prior to his arrival in Lexington, Singleton had been whipper-in to Mr. Thomas's Hounds and the Millbrook Hunt of New York, both of which were hunted by J.B. Thomas and his huntsman, Charles Carver. As his son, Rudolph Singleton Jr., later recalled, Rudolph Singleton had grown up breaking and selling horses. At some point, he came to the attention of J.B. Thomas, who in the late 1910s and early 1920s hunted in Virginia. Thomas took Singleton to New York and then to Overhills[50] in North Carolina.

Leaving the employ of one of America's most famous and relentless foxhunters to come to Iroquois as whipper-in was a bold step, but Singleton had recently married and was looking for a permanent home and a more prominent role in the hunting hierarchy. It seems likely that an arrangement was reached whereby Johnson would hunt the hounds for two seasons and then Singleton would take over. And, in due course, that is what happened.

In 1931, Johnson left for Virginia, and Singleton became the Iroquois Hunt's professional huntsman. His promotion coincided with the election of a new Master, Edward Spears of Paris, Kentucky. Hanger's business interests meant he had to spend an increasing amount of time in New York. Unfortunately, Singleton's promotion also coincided with the worst economic depression of the twentieth century. To some extent, Lexington was insulated from the effects of the 1929 Wall Street crash—at least initially—and for two seasons, Singleton continued to hunt the hounds. But in 1932, economic circumstances tightened considerably, and he was released from his position as huntsman. His son recalled later that two people came to the rescue: Ed Madden of Hamburg Place in Lexington and Percy Rockefeller.

For a short time, Singleton was paid by Madden to ride around the two thousand acres of Hamburg Place, looking out for any damage or signs of trespass. Then, in 1933, Rockefeller offered him the job of huntsman at Overhills through the auspices of the estate manager, Mr. Bruce, also a native of Sperryville, Virginia. The Singletons and their son packed up their car and drove the five hundred miles from Lexington to Pinehurst, North Carolina, a journey Rudolph Singleton Jr. could still remember eighty years later.

One question remains: how did the hunting then compare with the way Iroquois conducts the sport today? For the most part, the early Masters and huntsmen at Iroquois opted for a combination of the two styles—English and American—as the descriptions of two hunts from 1930 and 1931 show.

> Lexington Leader, *January 1, 1930*
>
> *The final fox hunt of the old year was held Tuesday by the Iroquois Hunt, 35 persons taking part. The day was ideal for the sport and the hounds had not been long afield when Jess Hammond, one of the best hounds in the hunt's pack, gave tongue and the hunt was on. The fox made for Boone Creek, crossed the stream, climbed the cliff, circled back into the valley and ran straight to his den in the cliff above Grimes Mill. The run was one of the most thrilling and exciting of the season and was thoroughly enjoyed by the field and the visitors who watched the progress of the hunt from the hilltops.*
>
> Lexington Leader, *December 4, 1931*
>
> *Members of the Iroquois Hunt enjoyed a chase in the vicinity of Howard's creek Wednesday. The hunters met at the Locust Grove school on the Grimes Mill pike and the hounds were cast near the Kentucky River by huntsman Rudolph Singleton. After following a trail along Jouett's creek, the hounds were moved to the Howard's creek section, where a real chase was offered. The riders assembled on a hill where they got a view of the fox with the hounds in hot pursuit.*

In part, this method of hunting was due to the geography of the hunt's country. Riding through the creeks and cliffs near the Kentucky River was hard on the horse as well as a foxhunter wishing to see hounds work. But it also reflects the interests of the men and women who re-founded the club. As John Gourlay wrote of Len Shouse in 1929, "We really pressed him into service when we organized the Iroquois and he has been of the greatest help to us but his heart has never been in Foxhunting as we are trying to do it. He is what we call a hill topper and riding and staying with hounds has all been new to him." Shouse was an extremely accomplished field-trialer and his enthusiasm was fired by listening to his hounds.

But on occasion, the field did also follow the hounds, as an undated telegram from Frances Smith and William McDowell to Arnold Hanger reveals: "After two and half hours, fox tired and managed to go to ground in cliff with almost every hound there and every member of the field." As Gourlay's letter of 1929 made clear, William McDowell and Arnold Hanger were both "good cross country riders…and like to and can stay with hounds."

Hanger's efforts in paneling the country—with the help of Captain Hall—had been aimed at allowing the field to ride to hounds in the approved style. And while both types of hunting continued throughout the '20s and '30s, the new Masters were intent on moving toward the formal English style.

Right: William Preston, the first president of the new club, 1926. *Iroquois Hunt Club.*

Below: Detail of the 1904 hunt country map. This was a more modest request than Churchill Newcomb's 325 square miles of country. *Masters of Foxhounds Association.*

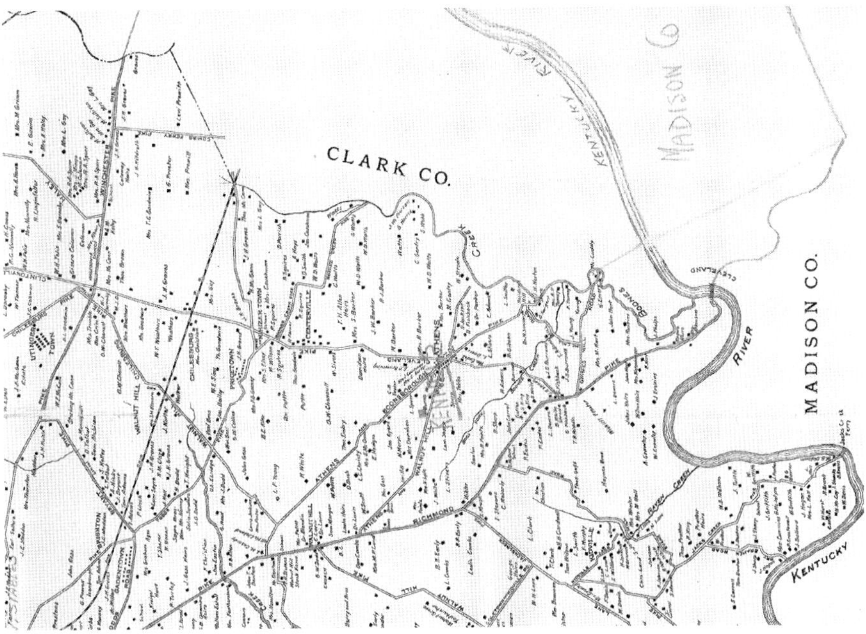

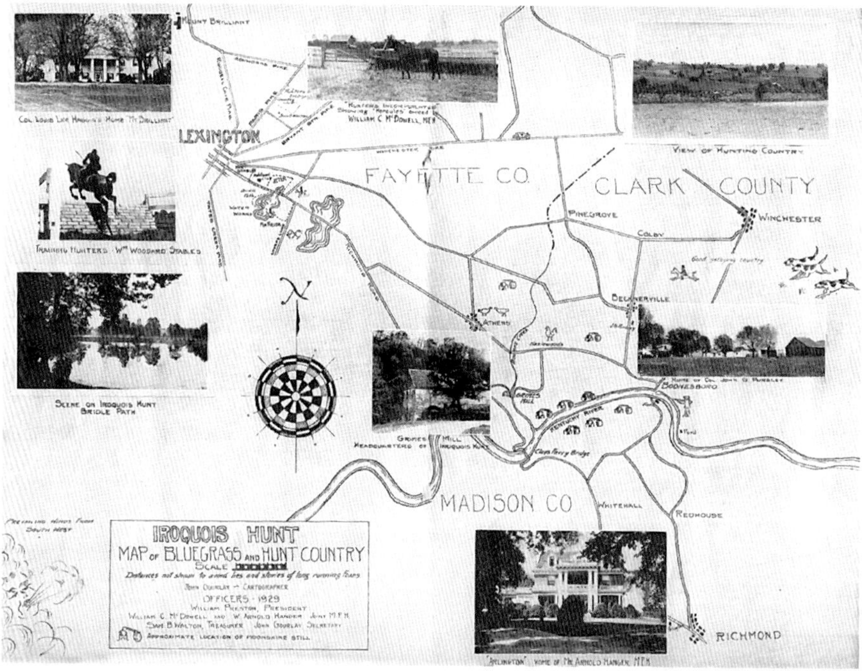

The hunt country map used for the program at the 1929 show included a Prohibition-era guide to the region's bootleg stills. *Iroquois Hunt Club.*

Blessing Day, 1933—*Plus c'est change, plus c'est la meme chose. Kentucky Digital Library.*

Above: Charles Kendall McDowell, MFH, one of the newly revived club's first joint-Masters. *Iroquois Hunt Club*.

Right: Leonard B. Shouse, MFH, provider of the Iroquois's first pack in 1926. *Iroquois Hunt Club*.

Huntsman Rudolph Singleton with his Walker and Bywater hounds. *Kentucky Digital Library.*

Foxhunters crossing a bridge in the mid-1930s. *Kentucky Digital Library.*

The paper chase at Ashland, 1926. *Iroquois Hunt Club.*

A meet at the Mill in 1930. *Mrs. Brownell Clark.*

Unboxing the hounds at Hamburg Place in the early 1930s. *Kentucky Digital Library.*

A meet sometime in the early 1930s. *Kentucky Digital Library.*

Right: Joseph B. Johnson of the Rappahannock and Iroquois Hunts. *From* The Chase *magazine*.

Below: Hounds going over a jump in the 1930s. *Kentucky Digital Library*.

Jumps in the 1930s. Arnold Hanger and Captain Walter Hall paneled the country and paved the way for an English hunt. *Kentucky Digital Library.*

Chapter 4

The Land and the Mill

A Place in the Country

To residents of Lexington, the Iroquois Hunt is often encapsulated in a single image. It is the picture of an old stone mill standing by the shaded banks of a rocky creek, while in the background, towering above it, loom the pale limestone cliffs known as the palisades. Grimes Mill, as the building is known, became the hunt club's headquarters in 1928.

The issue of finding a home had preoccupied the new club's officers almost from the start. As Churchill Newcomb wrote to Henry Vaughan in 1926, "The danger is that it will get out of hand and degenerate into an informal sporting outfit, such as the old Iroquois." But the idea had more to do with finding a suitable area of land over which to hunt than purchasing a building to be used as a clubhouse. That land would be known as the hunt's "country."

The pre-1914 Iroquois had been of no fixed abode and had hunted all around Lexington. Many of its gatherings had been north of the city.[51] Initially, the new club followed suit with drag hunts on farms near the Leestown and Newtown Pikes. But when, in January 1927, the Masters were invited to hunt near the small village of Athens, ten miles south east of Lexington, it became clear that the club had found somewhere it could settle permanently.

The search for country was not simply a desire on the part of Churchill Newcomb, Len Shouse and Kendall McDowell to prevent the club degenerating into informality. It was actively required if Iroquois was to be formally recognized by the Masters of Foxhounds Association.

And it was an issue the association took very seriously indeed. It was the need for impartial and binding arbitration in territorial disputes that first gave rise to the formation of the English and American Masters of Foxhounds Associations. And even today, hunting another club's country is regarded as possibly the most heinous crime of all.

As *The Encyclopedia of British Rural Sports* records:

> *In 1856, the Masters of Foxhounds met at Boodle's, a country gentlemen's club in London, and successfully petitioned the club's manager to establish a committee for settling disputes over boundaries and access to coverts. In 1881, a more formal body was established at Tattersall's, which eventually became known as the Masters of Foxhounds Association. This organization also became responsible for the publication of the* Kennel Stud Book, *which helped improve the quality of foxhounds.*

A similar situation occurred in America in 1905 in the aftermath of the Great Hound Match.

On March 7, 1927, Henry Vaughan, secretary of the Masters of Foxhounds Association, received a letter from Churchill Newcomb. Enclosed was a map on which Newcomb had encircled approximately 235 square miles of land that he felt should be reserved for the Iroquois Hunt. All the land inside Franklin, Scott, Harrison, Fayette, Bourbon, Jessamine, Clark, Lincoln, Garrard and Madison Counties—in essence, the entire inner Bluegrass—had been claimed. As a concession, Newcomb had excluded most of the larger Thoroughbred-breeding farms from his land grab. Even so, the aristocratic secretary was a man with big ideas. But he did not stay to see his plans come to fruition. And whether the MFHA asked them to think again or they simply developed cold feet, within six months, the Masters at Iroquois had grown rather more circumspect in their ambitions. In September, Vaughan received another letter and another map. This time, it was an old map of Fayette County (dating from 1904) that had been marked with a more manageable area twenty miles square and centered on the village of Athens.[52] From then on, the land outlined on the 1904 map was to be known as the Iroquois Hunt's country.

The land they had selected was already rich in history. Approximately 150 years earlier, it had been home to the pioneer Daniel Boone, who, in the early 1780s, left his original settlement of Boonesboro a few miles farther south and established Boone's Station. Boone's new home was close to the crossing point of two buffalo traces, a place known as Cross Plains. Over the next few decades, the buffalo traces were turned into roads (Cleveland Pike and Boonesboro Pike), and in 1826, the small town that had grown up around them was rechristened Athens, a reference to nearby Lexington's nickname, the Athens of the West.

Twenty years after Daniel Boone moved to Boone's Station, a family named Grimes built a mill to grind flour to sell to the rich markets in the South at New Orleans.

The Mill and Its Purchase

According to Iroquois tradition, Grimes Mill "was built for Philip Grimes in 1803 by a crew of Irish builders, captained by one Peter Paul." In 2002, however, local historian Harry G. Enoch—a man with a profound interest in the old gristmills of Kentucky—researched the subject thoroughly and published his findings in a book titled *Grimes Mill: Kentucky Landmark on Boone Creek, Fayette County*. Enoch's research showed that the mill was, in fact, constructed in about 1807 for Philip Grimes's son, Charles Grimes, and his partner and brother-in-law, John Winn Jr. If all this confusion sounds suspiciously familiar, it should come as no surprise. Enoch suspected that the original mistake over the date of the mill's construction could be traced to the same source from which emanated all the confusion over the date of the Iroquois Hunt Club's original founding—John Gourlay,[53] secretary of the hunt in 1929.

Enoch's book gives a detailed account of both the history of the mill and the people who built it. Like many families in Central Kentucky, the Grimeses came originally from Virginia. The first to arrive was Phillip Grimes in the 1780s. Born in 1734 near modern-day Leesburg, Phillip Grimes bought several parcels of land in Kentucky and settled on one of them, a 225-acre plot about two miles northwest of Athens. Phillip and his wife, Mary, were followed to Kentucky by at least four of their adult sons, all of whom settled in the area, bought property and went into business, though not together.

One of the sons, Charles Grimes (1771–1837), married into another Kentucky/Virginia family, the Winns. And in the early 1800s, he and his brother-in-law, John Winn Jr.,[54] went into business together. Charles Grimes already owned a mill on Boggs Fork, which he advertised for sale in 1804, but had clearly decided something better was needed. In May 1805, he and Winn purchased a sixty-acre plot from Eli Cleveland, who operated a warehouse on the Kentucky River that was used to store goods destined for the New Orleans markets. The land lay in a bend in Boone Creek about two miles from the Kentucky River, surrounded on all sides by steep hills and cliffs known as palisades which had been formed by the river cutting its way through the soft limestone over millennia. There was a long delay between the purchase of the site and the opening of the mill, caused by the requirement for a jury to decide if a dam could be placed across the river to divert water to power the mill. Thus, it is impossible to know exactly when the mill was built, although Enoch suspected that "construction most likely was completed sometime between April 1807 and April 1808." Nor is it possible to be entirely certain when the mill began to operate, as the jury met and gave its approval in 1807, but the court record was not entered until 1810. At some point between those two dates, Charles Grimes began to mill flour at the site.

As Enoch explained, in the early 1800s:

> *Kentucky was effectively separated from the eastern states by the Allegheny mountains. Because the roads were poor and the distances long, the Commonwealth's agricultural and manufactured products could not be gotten to these markets economically. At that time, the only feasible transportation routes to distant markets were rivers. Goods could be put on the Kentucky River and floated to Ohio. From there, the Ohio and Mississippi rivers formed a long, navigable highway, at the end of which lay New Orleans.*

Grimes Mill lay two miles from the Kentucky River and the warehouses that had been built on its banks. So Charles Grimes began an extensive road-building project to ensure his flour could reach the Kentucky River and the markets to the south.

Such mills were the engines of Kentucky's early industry. And before milling processes became industrialized and moved to the towns, the Bluegrass was littered with mills of every kind. The lower reaches of Boone Creek alone had at least six, most of them merchant mills grinding corn into flour for sale in New Orleans, rather than concentrating in the less profitable activity of grinding smaller quantities of flour for sale locally. They seldom operated alone, and their owners often concentrated several businesses in one site. Eli Cleveland, for example, had a gristmill, a sawmill, a hemp mill and a warehouse, all in one location, before the whole lot was destroyed by arson. Grimes's operation was similar. On the same site as the gristmill, there was also a cotton mill, a sawmill and a distillery.

As Enoch pointed out, although there is evidence to suggest "Old Grimes' Whiskey" was being produced prior to the Civil War, it became a more serious business after the war. By then, "most urban centers had roller mills that could mass produce flour cheaper, faster, and in far greater quantity than water gristmills." The war had also seriously disrupted the supply of flour to the markets in the South on which the mills relied.

By then, Charles Grimes was dead, and his property, including the mill, had been bequeathed to his widow and their two sons, Carlo and Charles William. The sons ran the mill through the Civil War years, when Roger Williams and his family left for Chicago. Two of Charles William Grimes's sons served with General John Hunt Morgan's cavalry and, while on a raiding party in Union territory in 1863, passed close to Grimes Mill. According to an article in the *Lexington Herald* of March 8,1928:

> *Anxious to see their father, they suggested to Colonel Cluke* [their commanding officer] *that they go ahead to the mill and arrange for a meal to be prepared for the regiment and with this permission they eagerly sought the old home, arriving late at night to the surprise and joy of the family. The next day when the regiment arrived great baskets of food were ready waiting for the hungry cavalry men.*

Despite overwhelming competition from industrialized mills, the Grimes family held onto their property, and Carlo was still there in 1880, when Williams is believed to have founded the Iroquois Hunt. But over the next forty years, the financial circumstances of the Grimes family worsened, and by the late 1920s, the mill had changed hands several times and was hardly functioning. The distillery, according to Enoch, had burned sometime before 1900 and had never been rebuilt. At one point, since it had left the Grimes family's ownership, a local farmer named Pursley had had a lien on it.

So when, in late 1927, the young son of the Pursley family—who was also a keen member of the Iroquois Hunt—informed his father that the club was looking for a home, Mr. Pursley promptly suggested they look at Grimes Mill and offered to underwrite the purchase, too. The officers of the club were quick to accept, and at a meeting at the Lafayette Hotel in March 1928, the membership voted to purchase the mill. John Gourlay wrote to the members later the same month:

> *Upon the practically unanimous vote of all those of the Hunt who accepted the invitation to the dinner meeting in the Lafayette Hotel Ballroom on the evening of the 7th instant, your officers have proceeded to purchase the Grimes Mill property for the use of the Hunt. In accordance with the plan stated at the meeting, the property was bought at the price of $9,270, and a holding corporation of the non-profit kind…was organized under the name "Iroquois Realty Company" to take and hold the title to the property.*

The purchase was underwritten by a loan of $5,000 from Mr. Pursley.

At first, the members thought they might be able keep the mill running, but it proved a forlorn hope. After they ground one last batch of corn, the machinery was disassembled, and Grimes Mill's days as a workhorse ended. The two mill wheels were placed on the lawn in front of building as ornamental reminders of former days, and Iroquois members donated items of furniture to decorate their new home, beginning the gradual accretion of objects that fill the mill's interior today and trace its history.

A Tour of the Mill

Step through the mill's front door, past the two stone foxes that stand sentry on either side of the entrance, and you descend down two stone steps—worn smoothly concave with the passage of time—into a dark, wide, low space: the central room of the club. The temperature is usually cool due to the thickness of the limestone walls, made from the same stone that towers above the club in the form of palisades. Around the sides of the room are sofas, chairs and occasional tables. To your left is a steep staircase that leads down to the basement and the former heart of the mill, and to one side is an old cabinet with silver trophies—the cups won by General Roger Williams at the National Field Trials before the First World War. To your right is a stone hearth and mantel, above which sits a copper plaque depicting St. Hubert's conversion. Around the hearth is a plain wooden fender, the friend to countless foxhunters over the years hoping to warm themselves after the chase. Straight ahead, across the expanse of wooden floorboards covered in Turkish carpets, is a bar with a large looking-glass behind it. For many years, Harry Parrish, the club's beloved bartender, stood there ready to pour whatever drink you liked—provided it was bourbon. But now his portrait rests against the glass instead. To one side of the bar, there is a strange wooden chest, divided into rows, each with numerous polished and unpolished brass nameplates on their doors. These are the drink lockers of the Iroquois members. Once a nameplate has gone up, it is never taken down, and the roll call of the club's past can still be found engraved here: Shouse, McDowell, Preston, Combs, Kittrell, Spears, Hanger, Van Meter, Pursley, Madden, Beard, Hancock, Gay, Williams, Van Lennep, Simpson, Mayer, Miller, van Nagell, Goff and Mason.

Around the walls of the main room hang paintings of horses—including one of Iroquois—and of huntsmen, as well as the hunt vest, whip, gloves and St. Hubert's medal of a former field master. And everywhere there are photographs—the paper chase at Ashland in 1926, the drag hunt at Shenandoah in 1904, the men who hunted through the war, the victorious ladies' polo team. Farther along to the right, an opening leads to the porch—first built in the 1960s and then refurbished to great acclaim under the presidency of Derek Vaughan in 2012. Around the top of the tall windows stand the portraits of Iroquois' Masters, presidents and hounds, and through the windows you can see the swimming pool, put in at the same time as the porch. Return to the main room, and you will see the staircase leading up to the second floor. It, too, is wide, low and dark. Two portraits of long-serving Masters dominate one wall, while a giant jigsaw puzzle of a hunting scene hangs on the left. The puzzle was brought by members of the Camargo Hunt to a joint meet and completed by Iroquois and Camargo members when bad weather prevented them from hunting.

Hot Bricks and Country Ham

Over the years, the mill has played host to some extraordinary events and characters: Prince Aly Khan and Elizabeth Arden at the Hunt Ball in 1954; Charlotte Pursley's horse Rafferty, the only equine known to have tried to take a drink at the bar; and a cockfight staged in a ring made from bales of straw placed on the second floor and put on for visitors from the North who had heard of Kentucky's reputation for such dubious sport. At least once, members have been stranded at the mill overnight after a sudden snowstorm. Mostly, though, the venue has provided an elegant backdrop for countless dinners, breakfasts and hunt balls. And throughout the past ninety years, Iroquois has been lucky to have employed some outstandingly loyal and dedicated staff, men and women such as Harry Parrish, Ernestine

Irvin, Eliza Johnson, Christine Gilmore, Gerry Hester and Debbie Young. Collectively, they ensured an extremely high level of service was received by members and guests when they entertained at the mill.

Naturally enough, the red-letter days of the club's calendar, such as the Blessing of the Hounds, are the ones that attracted the most attention. And given the dedication to tradition inherent in the club, certain specialties soon became essential if Blessing Day was to be celebrated properly. The full panoply of breakfast, as served in Eliza Johnson's day, was captured in 1962 by Mary Jane Gallaher for the *Courier-Journal*: "The thick oak door stands open, a fire beckons from under the large stone mantel, serving-men in white coats give the gleaming wide board floors a last buffing, and in the kitchen, Eliza Johnson, the club's treasured cook, can be seen busily readying the lavish breakfast that soon will weight the traditional hunt board on the mill's second floor."[55]

Breakfast began, according to Gallaher, with the serving of "Hot Bricks, a lethal mixture that look[s] for all the world like innocuous tea. Served in inexpensive china cups, it [is] made of Bourbon whiskey, boiling water, sugar, butter, and nutmeg." The assembled hunters and guests were summoned to breakfast by "the clear sweet notes of a hunting horn." The menu invariably included chicken livers and bacon, hominy grits, boiled egg casserole, fried apples, corncakes and sweet rolls. But the *pièce de résistance* was Eliza's Old Kentucky Ham. At least two years old, the ham went through a maturing process of considerable complexity, including salting, smoking, hanging, rinsing and scrubbing, before it could be cooked in water to which had been added "a quart of vinegar, a cup of brown sugar, several red pepper pods, All-Spice, and some whole cloves." Sliced thin, dampened with sherry and sprinkled with black pepper, it was served hot at the breakfast before the hunt.

Eliza Johnson might have long since left the scene, to be replaced by today's caterer, Cooper Vaughan, but the traditional fare served at the Blessing Day breakfast remains the same. And as the current club manager, Debbie Young, explains, it is not just the membership that loves tradition—the mill itself takes time to acclimatize to change. "Every time a new manager or cook takes over, the mill lets you know," she says. "The first year Cooper arrived we had a flood in the basement, and the ovens stopped working. I've been here behind the scenes so long that when the board made me manager, I thought the old place wouldn't mind so much. But no…it's acted up for me, too!"

The economic boom years of the mid-1920s saw a rapid increase in the number of sporting and social clubs throughout the United States. Lexington was no exception. Colonel E.R. Bradley's Ashland Club—dedicated to golf and fine dining—opened in 1925, just a year before its members re-founded Iroquois. Even so, the purchase of the mill in 1928 was an unusual step. Few hunts have a permanent headquarters, and most revolve around their kennels, if they have a focal point at all. Wittingly or not, the members were, in effect, continuing the ethos of the old Iroquois in the sense that the club was more than just a hunt. In the 1880s and 1890s, Iroquois had been as much about socializing as anything else. Members in the 1920s were perhaps more single-minded about foxhunting than their parents had been, but they were still a cohesive group of friends. The first two groups of Masters (Shouse and Kendall McDowell and Hanger and William McDowell) and the first two secretaries (Churchill Newcomb and Gourlay) had sought a country to call their own. Above all, it was the mill that anchored Iroquois to its country and gave the new club a permanence that General Williams's organization had never achieved.

Edward F. Spears, MFH, had an elegant façade that hid a devilish sense of humor. *Iroquois Hunt Club.*

Left: Harry Parrish, bartender. *Iroquois Hunt Club*.

Below: Prince Aly Khan, Elizabeth Arden and Mrs. Gene Markey at the Iroquois Hunt Ball. *From the* Louisville Courier-Journal.

Above: The victorious ladies' polo team of the 1930s. *Iroquois Hunt Club*.

Right: Spears and Pursley ruled Iroquois for forty years. *From the* Louisville Courier-Journal.

W. Fauntleroy Pursley, MFH, and hounds. *Iroquois Hunt Club.*

IH

List of Hounds

DOGS	BITCHES
Sam	Ruth
Crackerjack	Nancy
Jess Hammond	Peggy
Buck	Carolyn
Lucky Guy	Sue
Woodrow	Thisby
Traveller	Frances
Grant	Pearl
Rock	Joyce
Rambler	Alice
Leader	Sal
Bootlegger	Hornet
Quickstride	Dandelion
Rags	Tillie
Phil Green	Clara
Troop	
Hugh	
Sounder	
Charlie	
Ranter	
Ringbone	

Dogs, 10½ couples

Bitches, 7½ couples

Total, 18 couples

Fixture Card

Sat., Nov. 9, Grimes Mill, 8 A. M.

Wed., Nov. 13, Col. J. G. Pursleys, 8 A. M.

Sat., Nov. 16 }
Wed., Nov. 20 } National Foxhunters Association Field Trials, Nashville, Tenn.
Sat., Nov. 23 }

Thur., Nov. 28, Grimes Mill, 8 A. M.

Sat., Nov. 30, Hazlewood's Store, 8 A. M.

Wed., Dec. 4, Grimes Mill 9 A. M.

Sat., Dec. 7, Becknerville, 9 A. M.

Wed., Dec. 11, Greenville, 9 A. M.

Sat., Dec. 14, Hazlewood's Store, 9 A. M.

Wed., Dec. 18, Grimes Mill, 9 A. M.

Sat., Dec. 21, Grimes Mill, 9 A. M.

Wed., Dec. 25, Merry Christmas

Sat., Dec. 28, Col. J. G. Pursleys, 9 A. M.

W. ARNOLD HANGER
WILLIAM C. McDOWELL
Joint M. F. H.

The 1929 fixture card shows more meets and earlier starts. *Iroquois Hunt Club.*

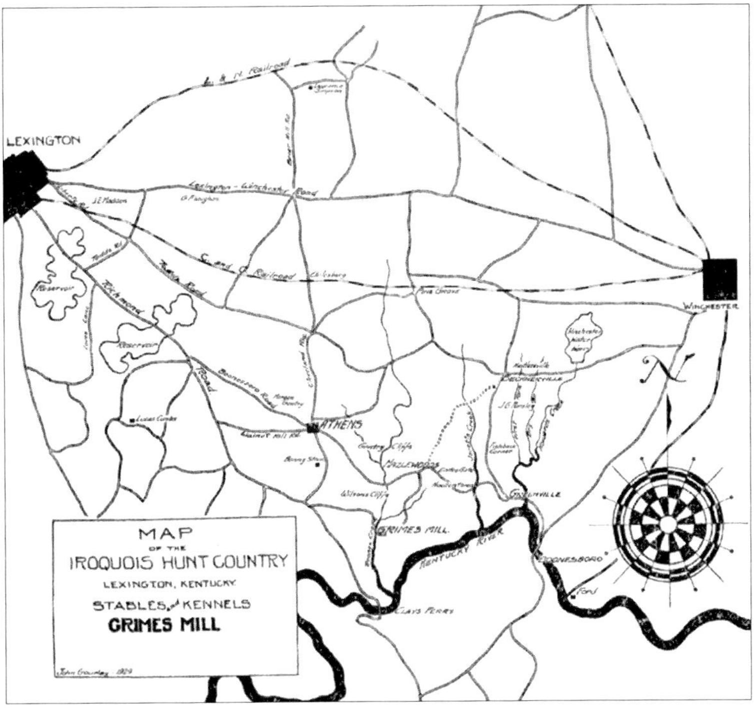

Inside of the 1929 fixture card. *Iroquois Hunt Club*.

Blessing Day, 1954. *Kentucky Digital Library*.

Opposite, top: Dennis Murphy and sons, three huntsmen of the Iroquois Hunt. *Mrs. Cathy Murphy*.

Opposite, bottom: Hounds arrive for Blessing Day in the 1950s. *Kentucky Digital Library*.

Top: W. Fauntleroy Pursley, MFH. *Iroquois Hunt Club*.

Right: John and Rena Niles at an Iroquois fancy-dress ball. *Kentucky Digital Library*.

John Jacob Niles, whose performance on the Appalachian dulcimer enlivened many Iroquois parties through the years. *Kentucky Digital Library.*

Chapter 5

The Golden Age

Ed Spears's First Day

In 1931, the club elected for the first time just one person to be the Master of Foxhounds, Edward Ford Spears of Paris, Kentucky, the county seat of Bourbon County. The new Master came from a family long established in the area and was a descendant in the female line of Brigadier General William Woodford, for whom Woodford County, Kentucky, had been named. One version of the Spears family history has them, like the family of General Roger D. Williams, moving to Kentucky from Virginia. Another version says the founder of the line, Jacob Spears, came originally from Pennsylvania. Both accounts have him arriving in Bourbon County sometime in the 1790s and record that he quickly became a famous distiller. In fact, Jacob Spears's whiskey became so good that he is often credited with being the man for whom the term "bourbon" was coined.

Whatever the truth about their exact origins, once in Kentucky, the Spears family prospered. By the time Ed Spears was born on November 21, 1895, the family owned several businesses, including a mill, a distillery and a thriving farm supply store. Although Spears was the only member of his family known to enjoy mounted foxhunting in the English style, like most other families, the Spearses kept hounds. The family also liked to travel. In 1922, Spears's father, Woodford; his mother, Elizabeth; and his sister, Mary, journeyed together to Europe for an extended tour of the Continent. Their itinerary would take them to Italy, France, Spain, Holland, Switzerland, Belgium and Germany. It was a significant undertaking, and they set sail from New York in April. In the days before passport photographs were a regular, and for some of us a painful necessity, each traveler's documents included a detailed physical description. Woodford Spears's appearance was captured at this time in the following way: "Age: 52; Stature: 5' 9"; Forehead: High; Eyes: Blue; Nose: Straight; Mouth: Thin lipped; Hair: White; Complexion: Fair; Face: Oval; Distinguishing marks: None."

It was a description that, in later years, perfectly matched his son, except for one category. In 1916, the twenty-one-year-old Ed Spears enlisted in the U.S. Navy, and while he was in, he is reputed to have had several tattoos. They were rarely seen, except on special occasions such as the masquerade balls at the hunt club—and even then only by a select few.

The Spears family had strong military connections—Spears had been named for his grandfather Captain Edward Ford Spears, who fought with the Orphan Brigade during the Civil War and whose letters home constitute a poignant record of the conflict. Spears, however, was destined for a life in farming and business, and although he liked to travel, he remained in Kentucky for most of his life. In August 1917, Spears married Billie Summers, also of Paris, Kentucky, and together they held court at a beautiful old stone house outside Paris named Harkaway.

Fortunately for posterity, two detailed descriptions of Spears's first day in charge at Iroquois still exist, and they help to reveal the workings of the hunt at this period. The first, an article by Laura Kinkead Walton, was published in the *Lexington Herald* of February 25, 1932. Describing the opening meet of the 1931–32 season, Walton wrote:

> *Very early, on the morning of the first formal hunt of the season, breakfast is served at the Mill and great is the bustle of preparation. The road is blocked with cars and vans. There is a thrill of expectancy in the air mingled with coffee and woodsmoke. The Master, Mr. Edward Spears, arrives early and he is seen talking to the huntsman, Rudolph Singleton, who has served the hunt so efficiently for the last two seasons.*
>
> *There is no loafing over sausages and waffles this morning. Vans are unloading and grooms are bringing horses from the stables. Soon the breakfast party come pouring out of the mill. A moment to tighten girths, examine bits and loosen throat latches and they are mounted. What a colorful picture against the stone background of the mill and the autumn color of the cliffs. Here come the hounds with their huntsman. They are a cheerful lot—sterns up, well together*

> *as if they know their business. Singleton signals them with a short note of his horn. Bobby Young (the youthful "Whipper-in") goes forward. The hounds follow with the huntsman slowly at a "hound trot." Next comes the MFH. He is the commanding officer of these scarlet coated thrusters. His word is law among them. It is his privilege to get mad and "cuss" a little if he likes, and if he calls you down, take your medicine and don't answer back. The rest of the hunt follows a hundred feet or so behind so as not to rush the hounds—for to ride over hounds is one of the unpardonable sins of hunting and deserves the black look from the Master it invariably provokes.*

A reporter from the *Lexington Leader*, who was also present, recorded what happened next:

> *Approximately 100 members of the Iroquois Hunt and Polo Club* [on] *Saturday morning opened the 1931–32 hunt season with what was described as the most successful and colorful cast and chase ever held in Fayette county. The chase lasted from 8 o'clock in the morning until the last of the hunters returned to the casting ground at 2:30 o'clock Saturday afternoon. Veteran foxhunters who witnessed Saturday's chase said they had never experienced such excellent hunting. Most of the huntsmen and huntswomen were dressed in colors. The cast was made from Grimes Mill, site of the organization's club house, and it was not long afterwards that the hounds jumped the first fox. This Reynard kept the pack busy for approximately three hours before he holed out of the race. Within a short time, the hounds jumped another fox, and this kept the hounds and hunters busy until 2:30.*
>
> *When the chase was called off and all the hunters had returned to the club house, Mr. Edward Spears, master of hounds, and Mrs. Spears entertained the members with a "come-in" breakfast. The breakfast was scheduled to be served at about 11 o'clock, but was postponed when such an excellent chase developed in the fields.*

After the breakfast, the new Master was presented with a silver trophy "on behalf of the Iroquois club as a token of the club's appreciation of what [he] has done toward the success of the organization." Inevitably, Kentucky being the home of oratory, a long procession of speakers then stood to expound on the merits of the chase and, in particular, the virtues of the club. They included J. Churchill Newcomb, who had returned from New York for the opening meet and who was to keep a watchful eye on the Iroquois Hunt for the rest of his life.

BLESSING DAY

One of the most interesting parts of Laura Walton's description of the opening meet of the 1931–32 season concerns what is missing. The riders breakfasted at the mill while the grooms prepared their horses and the huntsman readied the hounds. Then, breakfast over, they simply got on their horses and began the hunt. For the start of the next season, Ed Spears, ever the showman, decided to improve matters by introducing a custom that has since become synonymous with the Iroquois Hunt in the minds of generations of foxhunters and Lexington residents: the annual Blessing of the Hounds.

The ceremony is based on an old European custom and linked closely to the feast day of St. Hubert, the patron saint of hunting, which traditionally falls on the first Saturday in November. It marks the start of the formal hunting season and the end of cub hunting. It is not known for certain where Spears got the idea (in all probability, it was from similar ceremonies carried out at hunts in Virginia), though to some extent, St. Hubert's Day had always been celebrated—John Gourlay and Len Shouse produced a memorable invitation card for the opening meet in 1928. (And forty years later, in the 1960s, members would build a small church dedicated to St. Hubert in the middle of the hunt country.)[56] The first time the blessing ceremony is mentioned in connection with the Iroquois Hunt is in a 1937 account from the *Lexington Herald* describing the opening meet of the 1937–38 season. But the ceremony clearly started in 1932–33, as the *Herald*'s 1937 account explains that that year's ceremony was the fifth time it had been celebrated. The *Herald*'s account also serves to show how little the basic format of the ceremony has changed over the past eighty years:

> *The hunting season of the Iroquois Hunt and Polo Club was formally opened yesterday afternoon at the club's headquarters at Grimes Mill with the fifth annual ceremony of the Blessing of the Hounds. The Rt. Rev H.P. Almon Abbott, bishop of the Episcopal Diocese of Lexington, officiated at the colorful and impressive ceremony, assisted by the Rev. John Mulder, rector of the Church of the Good Shepherd. The ceremony was witnessed by a large number of spectators who lined the hill surrounding the club house. The Rev. Mr. Mulder opened the ceremony with a prayer, after the hounds that soon were to be the leaders in the chase had been brought out and had surrounded the old millstone used as an altar. Following the prayer, Bishop Abbott delivered his address and then after blessing the huntsmen,*

> *the hounds and the horses, placed the Medallion of St. Hubert around the necks of the hunters. Following the brief ceremony, the hunters rode to the scene of the first cast, which was made from the farm of Al Smith on the Athens-Boonesboro road. More than half the spectators present went along in the cars to witness the nearly perfect cast.*

Then, as now, the celebrant clearly felt under pressure to explain his reasons for patronizing an event some might construe as bloodthirsty. In 1932, Bishop Abbott did so by saying, "Respect for the past, the universal applicability of the Christian Faith, and the belief in the efficacy of prayer—these three and the sum addition is the justification, if such justification or apologia is necessary, of this service of the Blessing of the Hounds and Huntsmen."

In fact, probably the only clergyman to celebrate Blessing Day who did not worry about the ethics of the chase was one who hunted with Iroquois in the 1950s. And sadly, in the end, he paid the price for his passion. Despite the constant comparison of priests with shepherds and congregations with flocks, the hunting vicar's sheep turned out to have teeth. Incensed by his habit of rushing through services in order to get out hunting, they were on the lookout for any missteps. He didn't disappoint. One Sunday, in a rush (as always) to get mounted and to follow the hounds, the errant clergyman was seen to be wearing his hunting clothes beneath his vestments. Worse still, on his feet were not the sober shoes of a respectable parson but a foxhunter's top boots, replete with spurs. It was all too much, and the offender was removed to a parish far away, where such behavior was less likely to shock.

But as anyone who has attended the Blessing Day ceremony in recent years will know, between 1932 and 2014, almost nothing has changed. Even the parade for photographs was in place right from the start. In fact, probably the only difference between then and now is the level of erudition assumed by the bishop on the part of the audience. In 1937, Bishop Abbott could be confident the blithe references in his sermon to the hound Argos greeting Odysseus on his return home to Ithaca after his years of wandering would be familiar to everyone present. Today's clergy are altogether more cautious in their assumptions.

Ed Spears's innovation in 1932 was an instant success, and the ceremony of the Blessing of the Hounds quickly became a day for everyone, not just hunters. By the middle of the 1930s, the event was regularly attracting over one thousand spectators, and each year it continues to be well attended by people from the local community and farther afield. *Plus c'est change, plus c'est la meme chose*, as Bishop Abbott would no doubt have said.

THE IROQUOIS HUNT AND POLO CLUB?

Blessing Day was not the only innovation of the early 1930s. Throughout the early years of the club's existence, Iroquois members were active in helping to fashion many equine sporting pastimes apart from hunting. One such creation resulted in the hunt formally changing its name. In 1931, the club became known as the Iroquois Hunt and Polo Club.

Polo was introduced to America in 1876 by James Gordon Bennett,[57] a fantastical figure whose often extraordinary behavior gave rise to the British expletive "Gordon Bennett," used to this day to express incredulity at some egregious act or circumstance. At first, to quote from the U.S. Museum of Polo and Hall of Fame's website:

> *The game was a confusing affair that had eight or more players per side and matches lasting the afternoon. Over dinner one March evening in 1890 a few sporting gentlemen, including H.L. Herbert, John Cowdin and Thomas Hitchcock, formed the Polo Association, now the United States Polo Association (USPA). June 6, 1890, seven clubs joined the association, headquartered in New York. Soon, 100 handicaps were assigned to members, including future President Teddy Roosevelt.*

Roosevelt's friend, General Roger D. Williams, was among the early enthusiasts and tried to form a polo club in Lexington on several occasions—first in 1890, then in 1903 and later in 1911—always under the umbrella of his existing organization, the Iroquois Hunting and Riding Club. While the first two attempts ended in failure, the polo club founded in 1911—with Shelby T. Harbison as president and Roger Williams and Solomon Van Meter as two of the governors—took root. And throughout the 1910s, the Lexington Polo Club played games at various places around Lexington. The club attracted numerous sportsmen, including the famed racehorse breeder and trainer John E. Madden of Hamburg Place[58] and his sons, Edward and Joseph, and was assisted significantly by millionaires J.B. Haggin and W.E.D. Stokes. And when Harry Payne Whitney[59] purchased Greentree Farm, the town had on its doorstep someone who, in his youth, had been one of the world's finest players.

It wasn't until the mid- to late 1920s, however, that polo began to attract the wholesale participation of America's sportsmen. Kentuckians were not immune, and as polo fever swept the nation, three members of the Iroquois Hunt—Louie Beard, Frank Knight and Ed Madden—were instrumental in instigating the extraordinary popularity it came to enjoy in Lexington.

A native of Montgomery, Texas, Major Louis A. Beard (known as Louie) came to Lexington in 1925 to manage Greentree Farm for Whitney. Before that, he had been a regular army officer, entering West Point in 1906 and serving with the artillery prior to and during the First World War. Always an outstanding horseman, like many army officers of his day, Beard was encouraged to learn polo (like hunting, it was believed to inculcate sound military virtues, such as quick decision-making under pressure)—and it was through polo that he came to know Whitney. In 1923, Beard was a member of the U.S. Army team that defeated the British army team at Meadow Brook in New York. The match attracted a huge amount of international attention, being reported on in places as far afield as Australia and New Zealand. The British were overwhelming favorites, with their side containing several players of outstanding ability. Beard and his colleagues—Majors A.H. Wilson, J.K. Herr and W.W. Irwin—won with surprising ease and were congratulated in person by the U.S. Army's commander, General John J. Pershing. Two years later, Beard went one better, captaining and managing the army team that traveled to England and defeated the British army in two straight matches at the home of polo, the Hurlingham Club, near London. Beard played in the final match with a sprained ankle, a circumstance that left him with a permanent injury for the rest of his life. As the U.S. military attaché in London wrote to the War Department following the success:

> *The highest commendation is due to Major Louie A. Beard, Quartermaster Corps, for the efficient and outstanding leadership he displayed in training his team and during the playing on the field, and too much praise cannot be given this fine officer for the fine impression he created as the spokesman for the team at the many functions given them following the series.*

With the plaudits still ringing in his ears, the thirty-seven-year-old Beard resigned his commission and headed to Lexington to take up his post as manager of the Whitney farm, one of racing's most prestigious jobs. He quickly became one of the town's most popular and influential people, helping to found the Iroquois Hunt Club in 1926 and establishing polo as the summer sport of choice among the town's sportsmen. He found natural allies in the officers of the Lexington Cavalry Club, who, in April 1925, tried to establish their own polo team, and in John Madden's son Ed. By 1930, Beard had revitalized the Lexington Polo Club,[60] which was now based at

Greentree's Whitney Field, and made it a serious summer attraction. And members of his other club, the Iroquois Hunt, had started to consider creating a polo team of their own. The timing was propitious. A year earlier, in August 1929, John Madden had died, leaving his two sons, Edward and Joseph, the sum of $2 million and the two-thousand-acre Hamburg Place farm, three miles west of Lexington. Ed Madden quickly set about turning Hamburg into a mecca for polo. Throughout the 1930s, he would breed some of the most sought-after polo ponies in the world and would also supply members of the Iroquois Hunt and Polo Club with ponies free of charge.

By 1931, everything was ready. Madden had built three state-of-the-art polo fields at Hamburg.[61] In June, the Iroquois Hunt Club merged with an existing club, the short-lived Elkhorn Polo Club (which had been founded only a month earlier), to form the Iroquois Hunt and Polo Club. The combined team had just ten players at its disposal, and its first game, against the Memphis Hunt and Polo Club, was played at the Iroquois Hunt's No.1 field at Hamburg on Sunday, July 12. Sadly, the result is lost to posterity, but better records were kept of another game played later the same month by the longwindedly titled "Iroquois Hunt and Polo Club Shetland Pony Polo Team." Yet again, the *Lexington Leader* was on hand to capture the action.

"Approximately 1,500 persons witnessed a polo match at Woodland park Friday afternoon between the Red and White quartets of the Iroquois Hunt and Polo Club Shetland pony polo team," the newspaper reported. Despite the fact that the match was "the first junior polo game ever played in Lexington," it was played for high stakes, being described as "the junior championship of Kentucky." It was staged "with all the pomp and ceremony of an international match." The grass was specially mown to create a beautiful playing surface, official time keepers were on hand and grooms were ready to "cool off" the ponies and let the participants rest in between chukkers. The Reds won 5–4, with the winning goal "made by a pony which kicked the ball between the uprights."

Like hunting, polo was seen as a good preparation for war, no bad thing in the 1930s. It attracted the same people, and with it being played in hunting's off-season, it is no surprise that many hunt clubs took up the sport. Remarkably, in the face of worsening economic hardship during the Great Depression, polo somehow continued to flourish, and throughout the 1930s, crowds of forty thousand people would watch stars such as Tommy Hitchcock play at Meadow Brook. And just as remarkable is how good the Iroquois polo team became and how quickly it did so.

In retrospect, the 1934 season was seen as the club's best. "During June, July, and August of that year it became apparent that the club members were important to Blue Grass society and horsemanship," according to the *Lexington Leader*. The team was "runner-up in the Miami Valley Challenge Tournament and the U.S. Polo Association 12 Goal Tournament, after a 3–2 defeat by the outstanding Miami Valley Polo Club," a team Iroquois had beaten earlier in the year. A contemporaneous report estimated that the first team, which consisted of Clay Simpson, Ed Madden, Ed Spears, Goodloe McDowell, James Reese and Ellerbe Carter, played in front of a total of 100,000 fans that year. Practice games, played on the No. 3 field, often drew crowds of 2,500, while the major games were viewed by between 5,000 and 6,000 at a time when Lexington's total population was one-fifth the size of its current total of 300,000. Many of the games were played away, with the horses shipped to places such as Pittsburgh a few days before the game.

The club grew at a rapid rate. After three seasons, the pool of available players had expanded from ten to twenty-five. There was a ladies' team, led by Charlotte Pursley and Peggy Shutts, and a children's team, confined to the smaller No. 2 field and still running amok on their Shetland ponies. The facilities at Hamburg expanded, too. No doubt this was, in part, an exercise in "make-work." As the club's huntsman, Rudolph Singleton, attested, the Maddens did a lot to keep people from Lexington in work during the years of the Depression. By 1936, in addition to the three fields, the amenities at the club included a swimming pool, two "shacks"—one for men and one for ladies—to be used as shower and changing rooms, a croquet lawn and a bowling green. Huge grass mounds had been built around the No. 1 field and had been lined with limestone slabs to act as seating and tables for the hordes of spectators who flocked to see the games. They replaced what were known locally as "Madden's patent eye shades," literally large screens on both sides of the field that provided shade for "the eyes of one group of spectators and the backs of those on the opposite side of the field." Ed Madden had an inventive mind. The water from the swimming pool, which was close by the fields, could be used to water the playing surface as easily as it could be used to cool down the players and their families.

But despite all the growing success, the emphasis was firmly on participation, rather than victory. All members of Iroquois were encouraged to take part, regardless of their level of skill, and the club fielded three teams, with intra-club games taken just as seriously as matches against competition from outside. By 1937, the Iroquois sides were so good that "they couldn't find other teams capable of giving them a contest," and to stimulate interest, "the Maddens offered four Old English 'wine coolers' to members of the team who won a round-robin tourney," reported the *Leader*. The trophies were named for Pat Madden, the young son of the donors, and were won by Ed Spears, Fauntleroy Pursley, Ed Madden and Sam Walton Jr.

As well as one hundred percent participation, the club aimed for one other thing: the horses were all to be Thoroughbreds. Often retired from the track just a few months before the polo season began, the ponies, as they were now known, were retrained at Hamburg. The members were extremely proud of their mounts. After the first indoor match, played in 1935 and with just two players per side due to lack of space, the names of the riders' fifteen Thoroughbreds and their pedigrees were listed in the newspaper report alongside the names of the players and the score. The aim of using only that particular breed of horse harked back to the original intention of the fourteen horsemen who re-founded the club in 1926, which was in part to promote the Kentucky Thoroughbred.

Although the hunt would continue to be called the Iroquois Hunt and Polo Club until 1959, as Charlotte Pursley noted, polo effectively ceased with America's entry to the Second World War. Members today remember a time when the Polo Club on the Maddens' farm at Hamburg Place was still open to Iroquois, though no polo was played. In the 1950s and until it eventually closed in the 1960s, the Polo Club served as an alternative base for Iroquois members. The polo grounds might have lain empty, surrounded by their huge limestone and grass stands, but the swimming pool, lined by four giant gas lamps on either side, was used by adults and children throughout the summer months.

Keeneland

Although it was the sport of polo that first connected Harry Payne Whitney and Louie Beard, what prompted Whitney to bring Beard to Lexington was the management of his Thoroughbred breeding operation.

Racing and horse breeding had been Lexington's signature industry almost from the days of Daniel Boone. Boone and his fellow explorers and settlers brought with them hundreds of horses and noticed how they thrived on the pasture in the region. This was attributed to the limestone and calcium-rich soil and water and a particular strain of grass, indigenous to Europe and Asia but not North America, known originally as "English grass."[62]

The earliest races were held on Main Street and on Race Street[63] until the first racetrack was established at "Old William's Track in Lee's Woods...on the north end of West Main Street, now part of the Lexington Cemetery." Racing continued at Lee's Woods until 1828, when the Kentucky Racing Association began to acquire what would eventually be a sixty-five-acre site at the east end of Fifth and Race Streets, on which they built the association track.

The track had been the site of some of the original Iroquois Hunting and Riding Club's most memorable occasions. But by the early 1930s, it was in a terrible state of repair, and in 1933, it closed its gates for the last time. Over the next two years, Iroquois' vice-president, Louie Beard, and Iroquois member Hal Price Headley led the way in establishing a new course in the town. Polo might not have survived the 1930s, but Beard's other great innovation—Keeneland—grew to become one of the principal attractions of the Bluegrass for both visitors and natives alike.

On March 20, 1935, two hundred of Lexington's sportsmen met at Len Shouse's Lafayette Hotel and voted to appoint a committee of ten (led by Beard and Headley) to procure the funds to establish Keeneland. In fact, Beard and Headley were not alone among Iroquois members in moving things forward; a partial list of the initial investors shows that, among others, Len Shouse, Arthur Hancock Jr., Barry Shannon, Frazer LeBus, A.B. Gay and Louis Lee Haggin all bought stock.

While it seems obvious that the owners and managers of Lexington's Thoroughbred farms should want to ensure the town had high-quality racing to showcase their horses, what becomes apparent is a level of integration among sportsmen and sporting events that has today almost entirely vanished. The same men were often also foxhunters, polo players and field trial enthusiasts. One further example serves to emphasize the point. In November 1931, Beard helped to sell twenty-one mares belonging to Mrs. Payne Whitney. The sale took place at 10:00 a.m. on Tuesday, November 10, at the Lexington Sales Paddock. As one newspaper article reports, "The Greentree sale is one of the many which will be held during the annual hunt of the National Fox Hunt Association here the week of Nov. 9–14." What today would be a multimillion-dollar sale was then simply one part of a number of events that took advantage of their proximity to the main attraction—a fox hunt.

Spears and Pursley

For the first two years of his Mastership, Ed Spears was able to leave the management of the hounds in the capable hands of Rudolph Singleton. But in 1933, with the effects of the Great Depression having an inevitable impact on the finances of the club, Singleton was told his services could no longer be paid for. He and his family departed for North Carolina and the Overhills Estate of Percy Rockefeller. In consequence, the lot of the managing the hounds and the hunting program fell more directly upon the Master. Increasingly, Spears turned to a local farmer for help, an Iroquois member who would eventually become his joint-Master, William Fauntleroy Pursley.

As the *Courier-Journal* reported in November 1981, Pursley fell in love with the chase as soon as he saw it on "a golden afternoon of early fall 1927" as he watched "a dozen riders as they galloped across a pasture, jumped a stone wall and disappeared from view. Long after they had vanished he could still hear the hounds." Born on the family property, Nursery Place, "in a house built by his maternal ancestors at the end of the 18th century," Pursley had grown up in the heart of what was to become the Iroquois Hunt's country. His first sighting of the Iroquois Hunt gave him a taste for foxhunting that never deserted him. In the words of Rena Niles,[64] "A country boy, born and reared…Pursley had ridden horses all his life. But this was something else. He had witnessed adventure, glamour, romance all in one and he knew that he had to be a part of it." Pursley quickly learned the art of riding over obstacles—which, in those days, consisted largely of stone walls rather than today's wooden chicken coops—and soon he was "riding with the Iroquois Hunt, a group of enthusiasts who galloped after a pack of hounds in pursuit of a wily fox." In 1928, his father helped purchase Grimes Mill for Iroquois.

Although Spears and Pursley were only formally elected as joint-Masters in 1940, in fact they had worked closely together at Iroquois and were essentially joint-Masters throughout the 1930s. Pursley had been a whipper-in since the late 1920s and was made second vice-president of the club in 1931. When Spears and his wife, Billie, left for a 'round-the-world vacation in 1934, returning to New York from Southampton on the SS *Europa* in April 1935, it was Pursley who stood in as Master. From 1940 on, they ruled the hunt between them, Pursley taking charge of the hounds and hunting and Spears concentrating on the administration and the copious correspondence with the Masters of Foxhounds Association.

Physically and temperamentally, they could hardly have been more different. Whereas Spears was tall and slim, Pursley was short and round;

whereas Spears was unruffled and, to the Iroquois members who remember him, reserved—but always impeccably polite—Pursley was energetic and voluble. The word most frequently attached to Ed Spears by those who knew him is "elegant." In the memory of one member, he looked so perfectly turned out at a meet that "you almost didn't want him to go hunting in case he got messed up." It was hardly an epithet that could have been leveled at Pursley, who, members recalled, would often arrive in a rush, his apparel slightly awry and being adjusted by his groom. Once Pursley was hoisted onto his horse, his riding style looked perilous, but he was secure. In latter days, his wife, Charlotte, would instruct one younger member to ride alongside him in case of a fall—it never happened. He had grown up in the hunt country and knew every person, hedge, covert and jump, most of which he had built himself.

Perhaps Pursley's bullish attitude toward life is best observed through his name. Few men asked to choose between William and Fauntleroy would, if they were honest, opt for the latter, and it says much about his complete disregard of such things that he was happy to go through life known as "Faunty." As one member recalled, "He seemed to us the epitome of a foxhunting squire from England. Iroquois members would have followed him anywhere."

The Spears and Pursley partnership endured, nurtured by a close friendship. Neither man was a noted hound breeder or field trial expert in the mold of Len Shouse or Mary Combs or General Williams and Bonnie Stone before them. Both men were, at heart, farmers and tied to the land in a way in which the businessmen and socialites who founded and then refounded the hunt were not. Under their direction, Iroquois continued the pattern of the 1920s, which had been set by the divided aims of the first two groups of Masters and huntsmen. Both English hunting and hill-topping continued to take place, with hill-topping being a particular feature of hunting in the rockier river country. And true to General Williams's beliefs, the hounds were still uniformly American.[65] Under the guidance of the two Masters, the club settled into a regular pattern of life. After the maelstrom of the first four years, Spears and Pursley gave the Iroquois Hunt some much-needed stability.

The 1930s found the club at the heart of Lexington and the region's social and sporting activities. The polo team attracted huge crowds and regularly went on tour to other hunts and polo clubs, and there were often joint meets between Camargo Hunt of Cincinnati and the Iroquois. In 1931, for instance, members from Camargo came to hunt, stayed for a "breakfast" afterward and then went on to a banquet and ball at the Phoenix Hotel that lasted until the following morning.

As was typical in the decades before the war, the meets were invariably earlier and more varied than they are today. The 1928 fixture card for November and December lists five separate locations, including Hazlewood's Store, Greenville, Becknerville, Grimes Mill and Colonel G.W. Pursley's, and hounds moved off at either 8:00 a.m. or 9:00 a.m., with the meet often preceded by a breakfast.

Of course, such a happy existence had to end, and as the 1930s waned—and as the outbreak of war became increasingly likely—the two Masters decided that they must, at all costs, keep the club going and the country open. Doubtless they both remembered the struggle to revive the club in the '20s after the first Iroquois Hunt Club had fallen into abeyance under circumstances very similar to those they now faced. As gas, oil and other essentials became increasingly hard to procure, Spears and Pursley decided on their strategy. The mill would be closed for the duration. It would be too difficult to keep open anyway. But the kennel would continue to operate, though the number of hounds was allowed gradually to dwindle to about twelve couple. There would be no formal hunting—in the sense of dressing up in red coats, top boots and hunt caps or silk hats. Instead, seven men (Pursley, Spears, Bill Sphar, Clay Simpson, John Venable, Doug Goff and Ted Hardwick) would go out every week dressed in old clothes—khakis, coats and farm boots—and hunt the hounds across the country. Together, these men kept the hunt alive. And when, in the mid-'40s, the world began to resume its normal shape, the Iroquois Hunt was well placed to revive with it.

Chapter 6

After the War

Establishing the Peace

In such a short history, it is always tempting to begin with a reductive phrase, and perhaps the one most suited to start this chapter is: the Second World War marked a turning point in the history of the hunt. Naturally enough, the reality was more finely nuanced and harder to define.

On the face of it, the club was quick to get back into its stride. By 1946, the mill was already playing host to fraternity parties from the University of Kentucky. By 1948, the Blessing Day ceremony had been reinstituted. The Masters were eager to ensure plenty of sport was available for young men returning from the forces, and Pursley, J.E. Kittrell and a new member, Howard Tilson, launched their own expedition to Fort Riley in Kansas to obtain a selection of remount horses that the young veterans could use as inexpensive hunters. The club's finances must also have survived the war in comparatively good shape. In October 1948, the *Lexington Leader* was able to report in an article on that year's Blessing Day celebrations, "At present there are 65 family memberships, and the Hunt Club is supported entirely by voluntary contributions." There was no shortage of eager applicants, and as the 1940s gave way to the 1950s and America began to enjoy a massive postwar economic boom, the Iroquois Hunt had, for the first time, to limit its membership because too many people wanted to join. Over the next two decades, the hunt came to play an integral part of the life of the community around Athens and continued to attract interest from farther afield—through two annual events, in particular.

Horses, Hounds and Barbecues

The Iroquois Horse Show and Barbecue traces its origins to 1928, when the then vice-president of the club, Louie Beard, organized a horse and hound show at Greentree Farm. The aim was to raise enough money to put the club's finances on sound footing, and in this, it was successful. A crowd of 1,200 paid one dollar each, and the club made enough profit to finance a year's hunting. The following year, the show moved to Colonel and Mrs. Louis Haggin's farm on Russell Cave Road, and again the aim was at least partly financial, as the club secretary, John Gourlay, made clear when he wrote up the event for *The Chase* magazine.

In 1930, the show was held for the first time at Fauntleroy Pursley's farm, Nursery Place, on Jones Nursery Road, just off the Athens-Boonesboro Road. And from then on, Nursery Place remained its permanent home.[66]

The move to Nursery Place prompted major changes in the show's program. In its first years, the hounds had been as important as the horses, with respected figures, such as Jasper Maupin, being asked to judge. But by the mid-1930s, the hound show had been reduced to a simple parade of the hunt's pack, and a barbecue was introduced to feed the hungry hordes who came to witness the horse show, which now took center stage as the day's entertainment. The main event was the Roger Williams Memorial Trophy,[67] but there were classes for all, including children's ponies, ladies' hunters and horses likely to make good hunting prospects.

The farm formed a perfect arena for the show. The field in which the event was held contained a naturally occurring dip in the earth, rather like an amphitheater. Some jumps were placed around the lip of the bowl, but the majority of them were at the bottom. Competitors liked it because it gave them the feeling of having no audience to witness their troubles. Spectators liked it because they could park their vehicles around the edge and have a perfect view of the riders and horses as they competed for the prizes, provided they arrived in plenty of time. By the mid-'50s, the show was attracting so many people that the vehicles had to be parked in several ranks.

Gradually, the move to Nursery Place also changed the show's purpose. The need to make money had abated somewhat after the first two years, though there would always be an entry fee charged for people unconnected with the club. Instead, the need to thank the farmers and landowners in the area for their cooperation in letting the hunt ride across their land had become the imperative. In the decades following the war, the barbecue for the farming families became one of the linchpins of the local community; the show was regularly attended by crowds well over two thousand strong, and many of those attending were members of the extended families of the hunt country's farmers. As one landowner explained, "Although a lot of the families round here are related to one another, maybe they're cousins or kin through marriage, they don't get the chance to all meet up that much. The farmers' picnic [as the event was known locally] was the one time in the year when they all did get together and kept in touch." The show had evolved. The aim was to repay the local famers—both tenant and owner—for their generosity and to give them some entertainment. It was all taken immensely seriously, and most serious of all was the food.

As Rena Niles wrote for the *Louisville Courier-Journal* in 1958, "The Iroquois Hunt Horse Show and Barbecue is probably unique in that its success depends as much upon beef as upon horses. The menu seldom varies, and when it does, the variations usually lead to complaints. (The Year of the Burgoo is still remembered as an off year.) Traditionally, the bill of fare features barbecued beef, baked beans, potato chips, pickles, pecan pie and coffee." So, while the horse show of 1958 could be safely entrusted to the younger members in their teens and twenties, the food remained firmly under the control of the hunt's elder statesmen. As the saying goes, if you want to know what really matters to an organization, check which committee the managing director sits on. Ed Spears and Fauntleroy Pursley were always listed under "Food."

The preparations would begin early. To start, Ted Hardwick, manager of the Wellington Arms hotel, would order one thousand pounds of beef "from heavy corn-fed cattle and brought to Lexington on special order by a local packer," Niles reported. The beef was ordered in fifty-pound rounds. At 2:00 p.m. on the Friday before the show, the rounds of beef were placed in permanent pits at the Nursery Place show-ring grounds. The fires were tended all night, "the meat constantly turned and basted with special sauce." The meat would continue to cook until 11:00 a.m. on the day of the show, at which point it was "removed from the pits and the big job of slicing [fell] to club members who [were] to serve the meal." That morning, huge kettles full of beans covered in syrup, brown sugar and onions were fired up. When it was all ready, the Iroquois members who were not taking part in the horse show would serve the food. The Masters donned white chefs' hats and aprons, and lines several dozen deep would wait patiently as the plates were prepared.

The *Herald-Leader*'s Sue Fenimore Wahlgren splendidly captured the spirit of pageantry under the headline "Men Take Full Credit for Success of Famous Iroquois Barbecue Lunch." Luckily, she also got the recipe for the famous sauce:

> *Sauce For 2,092 Persons.*
> *About one pound of black pepper.*
> *About two cans of ground red pepper.*
> *About eight gallons of vinegar.*
> *About one box of salt (must taste for exact amount).*
> *About one pound of butter per gallon of sauce.*

In 1958, an estimated 3,500 people attended the show, and as Rena Niles noted, the "man at the gate ran out of tickets and had to write out slips entitling the bearer to see the show and visit the tables where the barbecued beef was served." The club was fortunate to have the services of Len Shouse Jr. and Hardwick, both of whom managed hotels and knew all about catering for large numbers of guests and both of whom were—thankfully—senior enough to serve on the committee in charge of food.

Point-to-Point

The other event that kept Iroquois in the spotlight—and in the newspapers—throughout the next few decades was of a more recent creation. In 1952, the junior members of the club decided to hold a series of steeplechases, known as "point-to-points." It quickly caught the public imagination. As Mary Jane Gallaher reported in the *Lexington Leader* on March 28, 1952:

> *Trailers laden with leggy geldings and mares, many from as far afield as Indianapolis, have been arriving all week in the Iroquois hunt country in preparation for Saturday's race meeting. Starting at 2 p.m. on the Athens-*

> *Boonesboro road, the junior membership of the Iroquois Hunt Club will stage Central Kentucky's first point-to-point races. Schooling has been going on for weeks over a difficult 14-jump course which covers three and a half miles, requiring horses to go up and down hill and through several deceiving streams. These creeks have already caused a number of riders, while showing their mounts the course, to find themselves swimming in full riding attire. Owners, gentlemen jockeys, grooms and their charges are arriving from Cincinnati, Nashville and Louisville to try for the trophies offered in the three races over jumps.*

Point-to-point racing is thought to have originated in Ireland sometime in the 1750s when, after a particularly debauched evening at the dinner table and the port decanter, two hunting gentlemen struck a wager to see who could ride fastest across country between two points. The points on which they decided, simply for ease of keeping them in sight, were the steeples of two churches in neighboring villages. Not wanting to waste any time, they mounted their horses and disappeared into the night, intent on their race. It took the equine-mad English gentlemen of the nineteenth century some time to put a gloss on this rather wild activity and, of course, to give it some proper rules. But eventually they succeeded, and the sports of steeplechasing and point-to-pointing were born. At first, the two terms were synonymous. But over time, steeplechasing came to represent the more formal and, to some extent, professional sport (including races such as the Grand National), while point-to-pointing referred solely to amateur races, which were organized mostly by local hunts.

The first Iroquois point-to-point consisted of four races: the heavyweight hunter, the ladies' hunter, the lightweight hunter and a flat race. The course was laid out on another part of the Pursley farm, in the fields behind Hazlewood's Store opposite the turn onto Grimes Mill Road. The aim was to encourage foxhunting, and the horses that took part had to be affiliated with a particular hunt. Their owners were required to provide certificates signed by the Masters of their hunts stating the horses had been qualified through hunting.

While the horse show and barbecue was principally intended for the local community (though it also attracted a great many competitors from elsewhere), the point-to-point was part of a regional championship that included similar races at Camargo in Cincinnati and Long Run in Louisville. Riders aiming to compete in the major races across the nation would use the point-to-points to prepare their mounts, and consequently, Lexington racegoers saw some of the country's best jump jockeys and horses in action.

The 1950s saw an unprecedented level of interest in the Iroquois Hunt's annual celebrations and occasions, such as the Blessing Day, the horse show and barbecue and the point-to-point races. The Masters had been rewarded both for their tenacity in keeping the hunt alive during the war and their alacrity in reviving the hunt's full range of activities as soon as possible at the end of the conflict. But the everyday purpose of the club was hunting. And although the Masters were quick to resume the regular pattern of cub hunting and formal meets, they were also determined that the hunt needed professional help. That help came with the arrival of a family that would provide the Iroquois Hunt with three generations of whippers-in and two generations of huntsmen over the next forty-five years.

From Cork via Wisconsin: The Arrival of the Murphys

In the late '20s and throughout the '30s and '40s, newspaper reports of the club's hunting activities show that the preponderance of sport it enjoyed was drag hunting and hill-topping. The hounds would be taken to Hamburg Place for drag hunts, and the field would follow in the approved English style. The hunting of live quarry would take place through the creeks and cliffs around the mill, and on these occasions, the riders would congregate on a hilltop and listen to the hounds as they worked, unable to follow them due to the difficult terrain. That is not to say there were no hunts after live quarry that resembled an English hunt, but they were certainly not the norm.

This style of hunting was also reflected in the huntsmen the club employed. Captain Walter Hall might have found it all a little unusual, accustomed as he was to hunting with the Border Hunt in the north of England, but he stayed for just one season. Joseph Johnson and Len Shouse were both enthusiastic field trial men and happy to let their hounds work with minimal supervision. Rudolph Singleton and Churchill Newcomb were fans of both types of hunting, English and American, in equal measure. Ed Spears and Fauntleroy Pursley continued the practice of hill-topping. Pursley's daughter, Joan Mayer, recalled, "Maybe a whip or two would follow the hounds, but the rest of us would stay on the hill and listen. And, oh, it was cold!"

With the departure of the last professional huntsman in 1933, Spears and Pursley took personal responsibility for hunting the hounds. They employed a kennel man to look after feeding and getting the hounds to the meet. The longest serving of these was Dave Tadlock, who was described by Joan Mayer as "a good old country boy who kept a few hounds of his own and would look after the Iroquois pack and haul them up to the meet in his truck." Soon after the war, however, the Masters decided that new professionals were needed. So, in the late 1940s, Iroquois members made ready to welcome into their midst a family of huntsmen who were more used to the English methods and who, with the Masters' approval, started to alter both the style of the hunt and the breeding of the hounds.

Dennis Murphy and his sons Daniel (always known as Bud) and Pat arrived from Wisconsin in 1948. Dennis was originally from a small rural community in County Cork, Ireland, where he had whipped in to the local pack. In the 1920s, he immigrated to America and, like thousands of other Irish immigrants, gravitated to Chicago. Soon after his arrival, he got a job as huntsman to the Long Meadow Hunt, just outside the city. But like Rudolph Singleton at Iroquois, Dennis Murphy found himself forced to move on as the Great Depression tightened its grip on the purse strings of Chicago's sportsmen. He got work as the huntsman at the Milwaukee Hunt Club of Racine, Wisconsin. Years later, his son Pat recalled the time he spent working with his father and the hounds in the bitter northern winters: "In the winter, we'd take them out and track them in the snow. My dad used to take the hounds out in his car, and one day the car got stuck across some railroad tracks. He had four or five in the trunk, I guess. He got them out okay and ran up the tracks trying to flag down the train. So the hounds were all fine, but we lost the car."

In 1947, Dennis Murphy came south to look at horses. His trip took him to Lexington, and while he was there, he met Fauntleroy Pursley, who offered him the position of professional kennel huntsman at Iroquois. Pat remembered the visit he and his father made to check out the small hunt in the wilds of Kentucky: "We came out with the hound truck when they let all the hounds out, we checked out the stables and we drove all around the country. When we finally got back home to Wisconsin, Mother asked us what the huntsman's house looked like. I looked at Dad, and Dad looked at me—we had never even looked at the house." Dennis Murphy accepted the job. As Pat explained, "My father fell in love with this country. It reminded him of Ireland." The family moved to Iroquois for the start of the 1948–49 season.

The role Dennis Murphy had accepted was that of kennel huntsman. It was demanding, to say the least, and had not changed fundamentally since the days of Joe Johnson and Rudolph Singleton. The kennel was next to the huntsman's house, opposite the mill. It contained forty couple of Walker hounds. The hunt horses were stabled in a nearby barn, and members could opt to have their own horses stabled there, too. Many chose to do so, and the horses—often as many as a dozen—were kept in lean-to stalls ranged along the outside walls of the barn. On hunt days, the kennel huntsman had to not only prepare the hounds and take them to the meet but also to prepare the Masters', staff and members' horses and get them to the meet. Often this involved a hack of five or six miles, with boys from the surrounding farms employed to ride one horse and lead three. Fortunately, they did not have to contend with the traffic that now plagues the roads through the hunt country, but it still seems like a lot of work. At the end of the day, the whole process was reversed, with the Masters and members dismounting at the meet—often Witt's Store (formerly Hazlewood's Store) on the Athens-Boonesboro Road, opposite the turn for Grimes Mill Road and a paddock that is today known as The Corners—and the kennel huntsman and his assistants leading the tired horses and hounds all the way back to the kennel and barn at the mill. Their work was not done then, for every horse had to be washed, and the horses and hounds had to be fed.

The work did not let up much in the off-season. The hound training program in the summer months was equally time-consuming. From the days of Roger Williams, the majority of the hounds at the Iroquois Hunt had always been American Walkers. Successive huntsmen found them good hunters but extremely hard to train, bred as they were to be highly independent and to work alone. Williams acknowledged as much in 1905, writing in his book, *Horse and Hound*, "The English hounds seem more susceptible to training and handling, as is evidenced by their behavior and good manners in the kennels and en route to and from covert."[68] Training had to begin early in a hound's life, and older hounds who could no longer hunt were often imported from other clubs and coupled[69] to puppies to help teach them the ropes. As Pat Murphy recalled many years later in *The Chronicle of the Horse*, "Back then the hounds weren't pack broke. You'd just take them all out in a truck and turn them loose, and off they'd go. We had a tough couple of summers out there trying to pack break those hounds. There were six- and seven-year-old hounds that had never been handled. But we got it done."

The Murphy family helped discipline the hunt both in terms of training the hounds to hunt as a pack—and making sure they returned to the kennel as a pack at the end of each hunt—and also during the hunts themselves. Before Dennis arrived, the Masters had been content to allow the kennel man, Dave Tadlock, to unbox the hounds at the first covert and then let things proceed from there, with little instruction given to the hounds by the Masters-cum-huntsmen. Dennis, Bud and Pat all made sure that the hounds were given some direction during the hunt. This had to be done surreptitiously, at least until Pat was made the official professional huntsman in 1969, because nominally, at least, the Masters were hunting the hounds themselves. Having experts on hand who could ride and assist with the hounds allowed the Masters more time to direct the activities of the field, to socialize and, more importantly, to simply enjoy the hunt.

Dennis Murphy's tenure at Iroquois was comparatively short. He stayed for five years before leaving to train racehorses. Pat went, too, and for a time became a successful steeplechase rider in New York. So, for several seasons after Dennis's departure, Bud Murphy worked as kennel huntsman at Iroquois. But in 1958, Bud was offered the chance of promotion and the job of huntsman at the wealthy Mill Creek Hunt, forty miles north of Chicago. And in another turn of the ever-revolving Murphy family wheel, Pat returned from New York and took his brother's place in charge of the Iroquois hounds. The job and the man fitted together like hand and glove, and Pat Murphy stayed at Iroquois for the next thirty-five years, first as kennel huntsman and then, from 1969 to 1993, as the first professional to be appointed huntsman to the club since Rudolph Singleton in the 1930s.

First and foremost, Pat Murphy was a horseman. At the riding ring in the paddock opposite the mill, he trained the hunt horses and taught many of the hunt members' children how to ride. There was nothing he couldn't train and nothing he couldn't ride, and his daughter Cathy inherited his ability with all kinds of horses. But Pat's great innovation at Iroquois concerned the hounds. Almost as soon as the Murphy family arrived from Wisconsin in 1948, Dennis Murphy had identified the need to reduce the influence of Walker hounds in the pack. Neither Dennis nor Bud had had time to accomplish it. It was Pat Murphy who orchestrated the change. With the consent and assistance of Fauntleroy Pursley, Pat Murphy started to completely alter the composition of the pack, which had remained unchanged for the past thirty years.[70] His first season, 1958–59, saw an influx of fourteen couple of crossbred hounds. The aim was "to keep just one-quarter Walker blood in the hounds" to help get a more biddable pack, according to Pat. The new hounds came in drafts from the Piedmont and Orange County hunts in Virginia. And over the next two years, the changes continued so that by the early 1960s, the Walker strain had been almost completely replaced by crossbreds.

Charlotte Pursley, Field Master

If Mr. Pursley was the one who ran the hunt, Mrs. Pursley was the electricity that made him go!
—Iroquois Hunt member

While Spears and Pursley continued as joint-Masters and Pat Murphy took care of the hounds, one person, in particular, took charge of the field and became responsible for teaching generations of riders the etiquette, manners and horsemanship required to be a member of the hunt.

Charlotte Pursley, whose name runs through the history of the Iroquois Hunt Club like Boone Creek through the hunt country, was never anything other than central to the success of the club. But from the 1950s until the mid-1970s, Charlotte Pursley's involvement provided the Iroquois Hunt Club with the most effective field master in its history. As one member recalled, "The rumor was that she carried a revolver about her person, and we all knew she knew how to use it!" Passing the field master was not allowed, and woe betide anyone who tried. She could, however, be oblique in her methods. Iroquois member Kay Holloway recalled Pursley berating her for riding too close behind. After the hunt, Holloway approached her to apologize. "Don't worry!" Pursley replied. "You were in the perfect spot, but those young girls were at fault. I shouted at you so they would learn and because I knew you would forgive me!"

She was born Charlotte Bowman in 1908. One of her mother's best friends was General Williams's daughter, Mrs. Lucas B. Combs; Charlotte's mother had often gone drag hunting with Mary Combs and the old Iroquois Hunting and Riding Club at Solomon Van Meter's place, Shenandoah Hall. Through Mary Combs, Charlotte Bowman got involved in the first drag hunt of the newly revived Iroquois Hunt on Thanksgiving Day 1926, which was in reality more of a gallop with hounds loosely attached. (The Masters and members alike were still getting a feel for the new sport.) As she recalled in 2002 in an oral history recorded for the University of Kentucky by Iroquois members Joe Jones and Lucy Breathitt: "Mary Combs knew I liked horses and riding and arranged for me to go on the hunt. I was given a horse from the cavalry remount section. I didn't know too much about what was going on, so I stayed to one side. After about thirty minutes of riding, I started to get ahead and people started waving me on saying, 'Go on, go on!' It turned out I had won. They gave me a little book about foxhunting. And that was my first day with Iroquois."

Like many, her recollections of the hunt, at least in the early years, centered on riding. She took little notice of the hounds. She did, however, take notice of a young whipper-in named Fauntleroy Pursley, whom she married on September 14, 1929. The couple had two daughters, Joan and Elizabeth, who would, in their turn, prove essential to the hunt, one as a whipper-in and Master and the other as an immensely supportive landowner.

A fearless and impeccably elegant rider, Charlotte Pursley, as she was now known, was the star of many of the hunt's equestrian activities, including the women's polo team and the inaugural Horse and Hound Show in 1928. She was also brave. In 1972, the *Herald-Leader* printed an article celebrating her twenty-five years of service to the hunt as field master. The author explained that

> *in 1939 Mrs. Pursley was thrown when a chicken flew from a ditch in front of her horse. Mrs. Pursley landed on a black top road. She suffered a broken neck, and after a delicate operation, was placed in a leather neck brace for four months. Doctors warned her not to attempt riding again. She heeded their advice until her daughter Joan expressed a desire to fox hunt. She returned to ride as a member of the field, guiding her daughter in the skills of the sport. Her efforts were rewarded when Mrs. Joan Pursley Mayer was named honorary whipper-in for the Iroquois Hunt.*

On another occasion

> *during a hunt when rain had brought creeks up out of their banks…the hunt reached a point where it was forced to cross a swift-running stream to continue the chase. Mrs. Pursley guided her horse into the rushing waters. After observing the depth of the waters, other members of the hunt moved downstream in search of a safer crossing. At mid-stream Mrs. Pursley's horse lost his footing, and she was thrown into the icy creek.*

In her own recollection, as she swept past the other hunters, who looked on helplessly, Pursley distinctly heard her husband, Fauntleroy, say, "Gone away!" though others thought it sounded more like, "Well, she can swim, so no doubt we'll see her again." That incident didn't stop her, and three days later, she was back in the saddle at the next meet of the hunt.

In fact, very little stopped Charlotte Pursley. Her daughter Joan recalled, "My sister and I had been invited to take our Shetland ponies to Hamburg Place to stay with our friends Preston and Patrick Madden. Well, Daddy wouldn't think of using the horsebox to take those two little things, and said no. So my mother put my pony in the back of her car and drove it to Hamburg Place. Then, she drove home, collected my sister's pony, and drove it there, too. We had a wonderful time!"

Charlotte Pursley's talents were not confined to riding. In middle age, she decided to take up woodworking—her first set of tools were lent to her by Iroquois member and future Master Jimmy Allen—and she quickly became extremely skilled, making fireplace fenders, dining tables, chests of drawers and anything else that caught her eye. Completely self-taught, she would spy a piece of furniture at someone's house, and in an instant, out would come the measuring tape and notebook. Many of the smaller pieces at the mill came from the Pursley workshop, and her daughters' houses are filled with beautiful pieces of furniture made by their mother. Sadly, in 2002, Fauntleroy and Charlotte Pursley's house on Cool Springs Farm was destroyed by fire, and along with the family heirlooms accumulated over two centuries by the Pursleys and the Bowmans, many works by Charlotte Pursley were also lost.

The Death of a Master

This chapter began with a tentative attempt to suggest that although the club seemed quick to resume its activities in 1946, the years of the Second World War nevertheless changed it in some way. The hunt was kept alive between 1942 and 1946 thanks to the efforts of the two Masters and their friends. Soon after 1946, the usual rituals of cub hunting, Blessing Day, hunt balls and farmers' picnics were in place again. But almost immediately thereafter, it is possible to detect a change—a tone of nostalgia—beginning to permeate newspaper articles reporting the club's activities. In January 1953, the *Lexington Leader* looked back on the demise of the polo team, saying the clubrooms at Hamburg had become "a place to reminisce about a Blue Grass sport that died." And increasingly, the reports started to emphasize the tradition, the heritage and what was being preserved, rather than what was being created. Of course, all that might be more to do with the way the club was perceived from the outside and nothing to do with the war. In the few years of the club's existence before the outbreak of hostilities, it had been at the center of a torrent of activity. Six Masters, five huntsmen, a polo team, a horse and hound show, new stables, a new kennel, the purchase of the mill—all this took place in a span of just fourteen years.

But as the decades of the '50s, '60s and '70s rolled on, only the point-to-point could be said to be new. And this, too, might have something to do with the personalities at the club. Churchill Newcomb, Arnold Hanger, Kendall McDowell and Len Shouse were all businessmen and used to constant change and improvement. Ed Spears and Fauntleroy Pursley were farmers, more accustomed to the steady continuity of the seasons.

By the late 1950s, Spears and Pursley were entering late middle age, and a younger generation, including Pursley's daughter Joan, was beginning to take a more active role. The men and women who had re-founded the club in 1926 were starting to drop away. Len Shouse died in 1957. He had been the hunt's first Master in 1926 and beginning in 1931 had been president for ten years. His hounds had formed the basis of the first pack, and during the Depression, when no other food was available, he had kept them fed with the leftovers from the kitchen of his Lafayette Hotel. In 1953, Charles Kendall McDowell was killed in a car crash, and in 1962, John Churchill Newcomb, who almost more than anyone else had helped to create the modern club, was murdered by an unknown assailant at his estate in Loudoun County, Virginia. But the loss that caused the greatest impact at Iroquois came in December 1970, when the joint-Master for the past forty years, Ed Spears, died after a car crash.[71]

Spears was seventy-five years old. The club went into mourning, and the depth of feeling he had engendered in the hearts of Iroquois members is reflected in the words of the plaque the members placed in his memory on the wall of Grimes Mill: "We had him so happily for so long a time that we had come to think him a permanent and inherent part of our Iroquois Hunt: and the sudden loss of him seemed almost unbelievable. He was an ideal Master of Hounds."

His joint-Master, Fauntleroy Pursley, was sixty-seven, and decided he needed to find a replacement for Spears as soon as possible. The person he chose was James B. Allen of Winchester, Kentucky, the owner of a construction and engineering firm. Allen owned land in the hunt country and threw wonderful parties at his home, Hunters Rest. Nevertheless, over the next decade, the club inevitably began to slow as the once energetic and unstoppable Pursleys and their circle aged.

In 1983, eighty-year-old Fauntleroy Pursley called time on his hunting career. He had been Master at Iroquois for forty-three years, longer than any other MFH in America. He had supported the club almost from the moment of its re-founding and had ensured it survived the war years when it could quite easily have folded. And in the decades that followed, together with his great friend Spears, he had built it up as one of Lexington's most iconic institutions. For his last season in charge, he and Allen had been joined as joint-Master by Bill Sphar, one of Pursley's oldest friends and one of the seven men who had helped keep the hunt alive during the war. Allen resigned the Mastership at the same time as Pursley, and the following year, Sphar was joined by two new Masters: Fauntleroy and Charlotte's daughter Joan Pursley Mayer and the honorary whipper-in to the hunt since 1969, Dr. James B. Holloway.

Three Masters, Two Views

Jim Holloway was raised in Lexington, but he did not hunt with Iroquois as a child. After a traditional education at Woodberry Forest, he attended Yale, where, as a member of the university's Officer Training Corps' Mounted Artillery unit, he was taught to ride on the horses used to pull the guns. It was a rapid induction, but he survived and became an accomplished horseman. From Yale, Holloway went to Duke University Hospital in North Carolina to do an internship, and there he met his wife, Kay. They married in 1943, and when he had completed his medical training, they moved to Lexington. Holloway began to practice medicine as a surgeon under the guidance of Dr. Francis Massey at the Lexington Clinic. He and Kay had three children—Elizabeth, Cathy and Blaine—and life seemed to be progressing on a steady path. Then, one day in the spring of 1955, a friend took him to see a new kind of race meet that was attracting a lot of attention: the Iroquois Hunt Club point-to-point. "I fell in love with it the minute I saw it," he was to recall. From that point on, steeplechasing and foxhunting became the Holloways' obsession. Soon Kay learned to ride, too, and all three children would become excellent riders as well. In due course, Blaine and Elizabeth (and Elizabeth's husband, Herman Playforth) would form the core of the Iroquois Hunt's whippers-in for almost twenty years.

Long after his retirement from medicine and the hunting field, Jim Holloway explained, "I miss surgery a lot, but what I miss most in the world is foxhunting."

By 1969, when the Masters appointed him honorary whipper-in, Holloway was an experienced hunting man. He, Kay and their children had hunted all over the United States and also in England. And in some ways, he harked back to the sportsmen at Iroquois before the war and, in particular, to Louie Beard. Like Beard, he was active in creating sporting events in Lexington that the whole community could enjoy, in particular the High Hope Steeplechase and the Rolex Three-Day Event at the Kentucky Horse Park.

For two seasons, the three Masters rubbed along together. But there were significant differences in the way each saw the hunt developing. Mayer and Sphar favored a continuation of the traditional style of hunting, as it had been under Joan's father and Ed Spears, with crossbred hounds hunted by Pat Murphy. Holloway, on the other hand, hoped to create a faster-paced style of hunting, similar to what he had experienced in England and in other parts of America, including with Ben Hardaway's Midland Hunt in Georgia. They had reached an impasse, and at the end of the 1984–85 season, Holloway resigned the Mastership. Although he would remain a member of Iroquois, his attention increasingly turned to a new hunt that had recently been formed in Woodford County.[72] As Holloway's daughter and Iroquois whipper-in Elizabeth Playforth recalled, "We lived in the heart of the [Iroquois] hunt country, and on Saturdays, while we'd see all the horse trailers driving in for the Iroquois meet, we'd be driving in the other direction to Woodford."

Back at Iroquois, Mayer and Sphar continued as joint-Masters for the next two seasons until Sphar resigned on grounds of age and was replaced by Bob Brewer, a local lawyer who had grown up as a foxhunter under the watchful eye of Fauntleroy and Charlotte Pursley. In 1991, they were joined by a third Master, Jake Graves, whose family had long associations with the Iroquois Hunt in both its incarnations.

Pat Murphy devoted thirty years of service to the Iroquois Hunt. *Mrs. Cathy Murphy*.

Masters and whippers-in—two generations of the Holloway family. *Dr. and Mrs. James Holloway.*

Iroquois hounds at summer hound walk. *Iroquois Hunt Club.*

Left: Joan Pursley Mayer, MFH. *Iroquois Hunt Club*.

Below: Jerry L. Miller, MFH, and hounds. *Iroquois Hunt Club*.

Lilla S. Mason, MFH, and Jerry L. Miller, MFH, discuss which coverts to draw first. *Iroquois Hunt Club.*

Left: Jack van Nagell, MFH, joint-Master since 1997. *Iroquois Hunt Club*.

Below: Iroquois Grundy '98, the hound that changed the Iroquois pack. *Iroquois Hunt Club*.

Iroquois members at Berkeley Castle, 1993. *Mr. Herb Sledd.*

Chapter 7

The Changing of the Guard

I remember the first time we saw a coyote in the country. Dad said, "That's it—that's the end."
—Cathy Murphy

When the Game Got Serious

By the early 1990s, Pat Murphy was in increasingly frail health. He had suffered a number of heart attacks, and it was clear that soon he would have to retire from the position he had held with such distinction for the past thirty years. And in the eyes of some members of the club, the hunt seemed to be ailing with him. The energy and enthusiasm imparted by Pursley and Spears were a distant memory. Several members had left to found their own packs or joined ones that already existed, particularly the Woodford Hounds at Shaker Village and the Licking River Hounds at Carlisle. Both packs were considerably less formal, moved at a faster pace and, in consequence, attracted younger members. And in some places, the country was beginning to be left untended.

But a more fundamental problem than this existed, one with which no previous Master had had to cope. Since its re-founding in 1926, the Iroquois Hunt had aimed to hunt one thing: red fox. Not indigenous to America, the red fox had been introduced to the country by the same English colonists who first imported the foxhound. The native species, the gray fox, provided less sport. Now, the red fox was under threat from a newcomer from the West, the coyote.

Believed to have started to spread eastward about eighty years ago (into the space left when humans eradicated the wolf), by the late 1980s and early 1990s, coyotes had moved into large parts of Kentucky, Tennessee and Virginia. Coyotes and foxes would not peacefully co-exist. In fact, coyotes often killed the foxes. So, before long, the only possible quarry, if foxhunting was to continue, was coyote.

The differences between hunting fox and coyote were manifold. Coyotes were bigger and faster and ran straighter, all of which increased the pace of the hunt. Members and staff who had previously managed perfectly well with slow or even slightly unfit horses now had to face the fact that they would be left behind the minute the hounds got on a run. Nor were there as many checks at which they could, to some extent, regain their breath. There was a clear choice: either switch to quicker, fitter horses in order to keep up or quit. Some chose the latter course, but most responded and displayed an appetite—and an aptitude—for the new style of hunting.

But the arrival of coyotes also created problems for the hounds. Traditionally, in the South and affiliated states such as Kentucky, the aim of hunting red fox had always been to chase, not to kill. This was possible because the fox posed no serious threat to the local farmers' livestock. Coyotes, however, are the single biggest predator of cattle (particularly calves) in the United States—and farming cattle is big business in the Bluegrass. Now, it was imperative to stop the coyotes from forming packs, and if a coyote was cornered, the hounds had to be able to kill it. And the Iroquois' small American hounds were simply unable to do that. Worse still, once on the trail of a coyote, the independent American hounds would disappear, often for days.

It was not the first time a new quarry had caused problems. As John Fox explained in *Bluegrass and Rhododendron* back in 1901:

> *In Kentucky, the hunting of the red fox antedates the* [civil] *war but little. The old Kentucky fox-hound was of every color, loose in build, with open feet and a cowhide tail. He had a good nose, and he was slow, but he was fast enough for the gray fox and the deer. Somewhere about 1855 the fox-hunters discovered that their hounds were chasing something they could not catch. It was red fox that had migrated into Kentucky from Virginia. The new quarry led to General Maupin and the Walkers developing their strain of hounds…* [Tennessee] *Lead was the first hound to catch a red fox in*

> *Kentucky. People came for miles to see the red fox that Lead ran down, and the event was naturally an epoch in the history of the chase in Kentucky.*

A group of senior members within the club decided something needed to change if they were to prevent what, in their view, might become the wholesale exodus of members from Iroquois to other hunts and the gradual financial ruination of the club. Their main priority was to find someone with the enthusiasm, hound knowledge and, most importantly, the financial wherewithal to revitalize Iroquois' hunting program. The man they selected was Jerry Miller.

To what extent Iroquois chose him, and to what extent he chose Iroquois, is difficult to determine. Perhaps it is more accurate to say they chose each other. Miller had grown up in the blue-collar town of Oak Hill, Ohio. The local industry was the manufacture of firebricks, which would then be shipped up to Pittsburgh via rail to be used in lining the kilns of the city's steelworks. It was hard, physical work and far from being well paid. From an early age, Miller learned the value of work and money. Many of the town's families were of Welsh descent—though the Millers were mostly descended from German stock—and like their relations in the coal mining areas of South Wales, the Oak Hill brickyard workers relaxed by playing sport and hunting. While the Welsh miners formed the Banwen Miners Hunt,[73] the people in Oak Hill pursued the traditional American alternative: night hunting. It was convivial, social and good-humoredly competitive, and the Millers were central participants. Within Oak Hill and its environs, the Miller family was well known for having owned some excellent hounds, and in Jerry Miller's uncle Jack Ward, it had a close approximation to a professional huntsman. "People would come from Columbus and pay him to take them out hunting," Miller recalled years later. "He was a real woodsman."

By the time Miller was growing up, the days of firebrick production in Oak Hill were numbered. Within a few years, a new method had been invented, and the brickyards of Oak Hill closed one by one. Education and then business provided Miller with a way out. By age thirty-two, he was a tenured professor at Eastern Kentucky University in Richmond. But finding the minimal workload unbearably dull, he decided to jump ship from academe to business when, in 1976, he was offered the chance to run the regional American Automobile Association club based in Lexington. During the ten years it had taken him to get through university and on the road to a tenured professorship, all thoughts of hunting had been put aside. It was not until the early 1970s that he had enough time and money to think of resuming his childhood passion. When he did, he turned for help to Kentucky's most famous night hunter and field trialer, Mose Hill.

"I think of all the hound breeders I ever knew, Mose was the best. When you have to breed hounds one year, compete and win with them, then sell them, and then have to go about trying to beat your own hounds next year, and that's how you make your living, then you're a hound man," Miller recalled. The Hills were famous throughout the hunting world for the brilliance of their hounds.[74] In order to follow the hounds' progress more closely when he was field trialing with Mose and his son, George Hill, Miller learned to ride. "I'd tried riding the draft horses back home when I was a kid, but it was just out into the field and back again," he said. "I didn't go to a field trial until I'd got my doctorate, and being young and adventurous, I thought, 'How hard can it be?'"

It was to stand him in good stead, though he had some unusual training methods. "The second horse I owned was called Faux Pas," he said. "I bought him from Eugene Freeman, and I think Jimmy Allen had had him at one time. He was always rearing, so I bought a small plastic baseball bat filled with air, and every time he did it, I'd pop him on the head. He stopped pretty quick after that."

Like the Man on the Whiskey Bottle

The only images of mounted foxhunting Miller had seen when growing up in Oak Hill were on whiskey bottles at Christmas time. His progress through university increased his awareness of the "alternative code" of foxhunters in red coats and top hats, but he was still a dedicated Walker hound fan, and night hunting and field trialing were what he knew. And under the tutelage of Mose Hill, Miller soon started to enter championship-caliber hounds at field trials across the country. The world of English hunting seemed remote and uninteresting. A business trip to Ireland changed all that. "We were there anyway and we thought, 'Why not try it?'" said Miller.

Soon he was traveling across the Atlantic up to three times a year to indulge his new passion, riding out with Ruth Hughes's Licking River Hounds at Carlisle in Kentucky and befriending leading U.S. huntsmen and Masters such as Ben Hardaway and Martin and Daphne Wood. He took with him a young Texan named Lilla Mason, who had recently graduated from the University of Kentucky. An expert horsewoman with few equals on either side of the Atlantic, Mason's job was to make sure the hirelings in Ireland were of a suitable standard.

As Miller's financial success grew, he started looking for land on which to keep his own Walker hounds and indulge his passion for night hunting. He had purchased a small plot of thirty acres in the village of Athens, ten miles south of Lexington, where he kept a few horses and employed Mason to exercise them in her spare time. Riding out along the lanes leading south from Athens, Mason had frequent opportunities to observe the land that lay within the country of the Iroquois Hunt. On one such trip, she noticed a 150-acre farm for sale on Grimes Mill Road. She let Miller know of it, and within a week, it was bought and a large barn was being converted into kennels.

Still, the intention was to have Walker hounds for field trialing and night hunting. Mounted hunting was separate. All of that changed one day in the late 1980s when former Iroquois Master James Holloway walked down the long driveway of Miller's farm and informed him he wanted to make him a member of the hunt. "I sort of knew who he was, but not really," Miller said. "He said to me, 'I'm going to make you a member of Iroquois.' I just shrugged and said, 'Okay.'" Nevertheless, Miller began to hunt with Iroquois, with Mason acting as his groom. And soon, as his interest in and knowledge of hounds became apparent to the other members, he was invited to become a whipper-in.

Miller was becoming ever more intrigued and through friends made in Ireland, he and Mason traveled to England to see how foxhunting was conducted there. They found a very different sport from the one practiced in Kentucky. Miller explained later, "The first day out, we didn't say anything. We just wanted to observe. Then, when we got back into the car, we asked the woman who'd taken us out, 'Okay—what did we do wrong?' 'Well,' she answered, 'the rust-colored breeches were a mistake.' She then took us apart bit by bit until there was nothing left!" Miller and Mason laughed at the recollection. Their guide, Philippa Coleman, future wife of one of the great English huntsmen of the last thirty years, knew her business.

"That afternoon, we went [with Philippa] to a tack shop," Miller continued. "We got all the kit. We wanted to make sure we'd never stand out like that again."

They also had a strategy. "We never spoke to the Masters or got on friendly terms with the higher-ups," said Miller. "Instead, we concentrated on getting to know the huntsmen and the whippers-in. We watched the hounds and talked to the staff afterwards about how each one had done. We were there to learn."

They had arrived at a fortuitous time. One of the most respected figures in English hunting, and latterly a friend to them both, was Captain Brian Fanshawe, Master and huntsman of the Cottesmore Hunt, one of the most fashionable packs in Leicestershire—the hunting world's mecca. In the late 1980s and early 1990s, Fanshawe; his cousin Captain Ian Farquhar, Master and huntsman of the Duke of Beaufort's Hunt; and their mutual friend Martin Scott of the Vale of the White Horse formed a triumvirate of influential younger foxhunters who decided to change the prevailing attitude of English Masters when dealing with American visitors. Many foxhunting Americans visited England each year. Most, in Miller's experience, were there to socialize and have fun. Occasionally, these visitors would ask for a hound to take back to include some English blood in their own pack. Fanshawe had noticed that while many English Masters were willing to give their guests English bloodlines, they seldom gave them their best. He and his friends were determined to change that.

As Miller recalled later, "I think deep down in their English hearts they reacted to the fact that I was very selective about hounds. I didn't just want to take anything, and I was thinking about the pack. I'd always ask them, 'So how will this bloodline nick in with the pack?' And I don't think they'd seen that much before."

Back at Iroquois, it was at first agreed to ask Miller only if he would be willing to act as amateur huntsman on days when Pat Murphy was too ill to go out and if he would take charge of the hound program with the explicit understanding that when Pat retired, he would take over as huntsman. The Masters—Bob Brewer, Joan Mayer and Jake Graves—had been looking for someone to help Pat for several years, and Pat himself seemed delighted with the idea. But one Master, Joan Mayer, was unhappy with the selection, fearing that the choice might unleash wholesale changes to the club and its traditions. Miller, meanwhile, agreed to the proposal and, as a former professional educator, realized that his first duties should be to contact experts in America, such as the Midland Hunt's Ben Hardaway, for advice and to show his new colleagues at Iroquois the profound differences in hunting, hound training and hound care that he had discovered existed between Iroquois and hunts in England.

As Ben Hardaway remembered in his autobiography, *Never Outfoxed*, Miller first approached him at a hound show in 1991:

> *Back in the spring of 1991, I was asked to judge the Midwest Hound Show.*[75] *Between classes a big guy came right up to me and asked, "Are*

> *you Ben Hardaway?" Taken a little aback, I said, "Yeah, what's eating on you?" "Well," he replied, "I want to meet Ben Hardaway so I can say I know Ben Hardaway. I've foxhunted and had foxhounds all my life and won a lot of field trials with Running Walker dogs. Recently I went over to England as I'm interested in helping the Iroquois Hunt here in Lexington, Kentucky, breed a fine pack of foxhounds. Wherever we went and started talking about foxhunting in America, the English would say, "Do you know Ben Hardaway?" I'd say, "No, never heard of the fellow." They would say, "Well, you can't be much of a foxhunter."*

For the second part of his agenda, Miller arranged a series of visits for several members of Iroquois to some of the most highly regarded English hunts. The visits took place during the summers of 1993 and 1994. While on the first of those visits, Miller was formally asked by a group of senior members to become joint-Master of Iroquois. In his recollection, he reluctantly agreed. The move, however, prompted the de-selection of the one Master who was opposed to the scheme, Joan Mayer. At a meeting of the board on August 3, 1993, Miller and another member, Edith Conyers, were voted in as joint-Masters alongside Jake Graves and Bob Brewer, and Joan Mayer was voted out. It marked the end of fifty years of continuous service to the club by the Pursley family.

To England in Search of Hounds

To the new Masters at Iroquois, one thing was clear: a different type of hound was needed if the hunt was going to be able to pursue coyote. "It seemed to me that the only people who could boast of any success in hunting and dispatching coyote in this country at that time were Marty and Daphne Wood[76] and that even though they bred their own hounds, their bloodlines originated in England," said Miller. Over the next few years, Miller and Mason made an exhaustive study of English hounds. "We went everywhere!" Mason recalled. "To the Quorn, the Beaufort, the Berkeley, the Belvoir." But it was at the Cottesmore Hunt in Leicestershire that Miller finally found what he was looking for.

Brian Fanshawe, Master and huntsman of the Cottesmore when Miller first visited, was born into the hunting purple. His father, Richard, had been a famous Master and huntsman of the South Oxfordshire in the days before the Second World War and had also won a bronze medal in the Three-Day Event at the 1936 Olympics in Berlin. In 1939, Brian's father left with his regiment on active service, and Brian's mother, Ruth, hunted the hounds in her husband's place. She was a more than adequate substitute. Her brother, Sir Peter Farquhar, Bt,[77] and his son Captain Ian Farquhar were two of the most influential and revered of all England's Masters and huntsmen.

Progressing from Stowe School to a short service commission in the twelfth Lancers, Fanshawe started his own career as a Master and huntsman at the Warwickshire Hunt before moving to Ireland and the Galway. From there, he went to the North Cotswold and finally to the Cottesmore. Tall, laconic and weather-beaten, Fanshawe was, as Miller recalls, relentless in pursuit of foxes and endlessly patient with his hounds, if not always with the people who followed them. His field masters—men and women not normally noted for their timidity—would hide from him in terror if they made a mistake. One enemy christened him "Galtieri" after the leader of the Argentine junta responsible for the Falklands Conflict. Even the Prince of Wales, who hunted with him often, knew to keep a low profile when the day wasn't going according to plan. But Fanshawe's hounds adored him. In the manner of many English Masters, during the season he did not have much to do with them when they weren't hunting. Nevertheless, they all knew who was in charge, and the story is told of one hound, apparently secure behind a ten-foot chain-link fence, recognizing the sound of Fanshawe's car as he drove to the kennel after a long absence and leaping over the fence in his joy at being reunited with his master, only to land full square on top of the startled MFH.

The Cottesmore hounds appealed to Miller because they were biddable, strong, intelligent and fast. "They handled almost like pet dogs, really," recalled Fanshawe. Above all, they needed lots of hunting and adored their work. "I remember coming in with the Cottesmore one day," said Miller. "Brian had made a pig of himself, and had stayed out 'til it was almost black. But as we were riding in, every one of his hounds was with him, heads up, sterns wagging. They looked so happy. They'd given everything, and they wanted to be with him."

One bloodline in particular stood out: the Carlow ST.[78] The line exemplified all that Miller thought best about the Cottesmore hounds. Fanshawe first brought the line to the Warwickshire in 1966 and took it with him to Galway, the North Cotswold and to the Cottesmore when he took over in the autumn of 1981. But as the name implies, the Carlow ST originated in the southeast of Ireland at the Carlow Hunt. It was supposed never to have left. The Master of the Carlow was Mrs. Pug Alexander, daughter of the redoubtable Mrs. Olive Hall.[79] When the Carlow Hunt disbanded in 1966, Alexander was determined that the ST line should never leave Ireland. Fanshawe remembers his father, who was living near Carlow, calling to ask if he wanted him to try to send over some whelps but being unable to get any. Fanshawe then called a friend at another Irish hunt, who he knew already had some ST blood. The friend replied that unfortunately he had signed a document that very morning agreeing not to part with any of it. Clearly, Mrs. Alexander was determined the English would never prosper from her mother's famous hounds.

About a year later, in midsummer, Fanshawe was looking forward to watching the afternoon's play in the Test match on television. As he recalled, "I got a call from my friend in Ireland, and he said, 'What are you doing this afternoon?' 'Watching the cricket,' I replied."

"'Oh no, you're not!' he said. 'You're going to Heathrow. I've sent you two Carlow ST pups, and they're landing there in an hour.' Needless to say, I got in my car and drove like mad to Heathrow." The pups made the journey back to the North Cotswold kennels in a crate strapped to the back of Fanshawe's vehicle. The Carlow ST bloodline would go on to form the basis not just of Brian Fanshawe's packs at the North Cotswold and the Cottesmore but also of Miller's pack at the Iroquois Hunt in Lexington, Kentucky.[80]

Sticking with their strategy, however, when they started hunting with him at the Cottesmore in the late 1980s and early 1990s, Miller and Mason did not approach Fanshawe directly. Instead, they got to know the professional whipper-in who had accompanied him to the Cottesmore from the North Cotswold, Neil Coleman. Neil would eventually take over as huntsman of the Cottesmore when Fanshawe retired—though as a professional, he was never to become Master[81]—and would continue to send drafts of hounds to Iroquois. After two years of visiting the Cottesmore whenever possible, Miller decided the time was right. "Jerry approached me one day," remembered Fanshawe. "I was aware he'd been out with us a lot, and I thought he was the quietest American I'd ever met! Finally, he walked up to me and said, 'I've been riding with you for two years, and you've never once spoken to me!' to which Neil, who was listening, said, 'Aren't you the lucky one!' I felt so bad that I gave him a hound to make up for it." Naturally, it had to be a Carlow ST.

The hound they selected was Statesman.

At the Third Time of Asking…

It is sometimes useful (at least, if you are writing its history) to look at the evolution of the Iroquois Hunt Club not as a continuous arc but as three separate stories: the 1880s to 1914, 1926 to 1992, and 1993 to the present. In each of the club's two previous incarnations, the Masters in charge had considered using English hounds and rejected the idea. Now, their time had come. So perhaps in one sense, the pivotal moment of the third story, after the accession of Jerry Miller to the Mastership, was the arrival of the hound known as "Peter," more formally called Iroquois Statesman '94.

Statesman was christened "Peter" by Miller and Mason in remembrance of a particularly English-sounding mother they had encountered at England's Peterborough Hound Show, who had constantly admonished her small son, "Proper yourself, Peter!" He was the first of what would become a flood of English hounds crossing the Atlantic to Lexington. Within a year of his arrival, and while he was still an "un-entered" hound, Statesman was crowned champion of the Mid-America Hound Show. He and his pack mates would demonstrate to Miller that he had been right in attempting to use English hounds to pursue American coyotes. Their success would embolden him and the other supportive members of the club to persevere and show other hunts around the country what could be done with English hounds.

True to his word, Fanshawe had given Iroquois a hound with an illustrious pedigree. By Cottesmore Faction '87 out of Cottesmore Storage '89, Statesman's lineage stretched back to Hugo Meynell's Quorn Hunt and a hound the father of modern foxhunting bred himself in 1784, Quorn General. Among his ancestors were Squire Osbaldeston's Furrier 1820 and Brocklesby Ringwood 1788, whose portrait was painted by George Stubbs.[82] Only one other hound—the all-conquering Grundy—had more impact on the Iroquois pack of the 1990s than the one known affectionately all his life as Peter.

At first, though, Miller had to move with caution; he had to begin by using American hounds. "Politically, I felt I had to try them [because] the hunt had such a long history with Walkers and Crossbreds," he recalled. So drafts were incorporated from Ben Hardaway's Midland Hunt, and while Pat Murphy entered his final year of hunting with Miller as his understudy, each man looked at the existing Iroquois hounds to determine which was likely to be worthwhile keeping. The Walkers and Hardaway drafts worked alongside the English hounds brought from the Cottesmore, the Bicester, the Berkeley and the Duke of Beaufort. And for the next few seasons, Miller tried to get the two sets of hounds to work together. He found, as he suspected he would, that only the English hounds were capable of running coyote and dispatching them, too. So the influx continued.

A Kennel Fit for a Hound

In 1993, hounds were not the only things that needed to be changed if the club was to be revitalized and returned to the success it had enjoyed under Fauntleroy Pursley and Ed Spears. For a start, a new kennel had to be built.

The old kennel behind the huntsman's house, across the road from the mill, had been put up by Len Shouse in 1928–29. It was in a dilapidated condition and needed money spent on it. As it transpired, it was also in a bad position, being close to Boone Creek.

Construction work on the new kennel began in 1994. Six months later came the first serious outbreak of a disease that was to plague the Iroquois hounds over the next decade. Blastomycosis, sometimes known as "Chicago Disease," is a fungal infection endemic to the eastern areas of North America. First described by Thomas Gilchrist in 1894, the disease affects the lungs of humans and dogs and can often prove fatal. It is thought to be particularly prevalent in forested and watershed areas. So the proximity to Boone Creek was a liability. Iroquois' hounds had been affected by a mysterious ailment for many years, but it wasn't until they started to receive regular veterinary care in 1993–94 that blastomycosis was diagnosed as the problem. Throughout the '90s, the pack suffered from occasional epidemics. But in 1998, there were over forty cases in a single season, and at last everyone was persuaded of the need to move the kennel. Several options were considered, but the most obvious choice was Miller's farm on the high ground about two miles from the mill.[83]

Soon the sound of hounds singing would echo across the pastures of Miller's farm. But there was an unexpected downside to the move. Since 1928, dinners at the mill had always been eaten to the accompanying strains of hound music. Social members might not always have been entirely familiar with the workings of the hunt, but as former Iroquois president Herb Sledd recalled, when you ate at the mill, "you always heard the hounds barking and singing behind the huntsman's house." There was no escaping the fact that Iroquois was a hunt. Sadly, all that stopped in 1998.

And apart from simple renovation, a new way of doing things also had to be learned. By the time he officially became Master in 1993–94, Miller had gained a certain amount of experience, at least through observation, of how to handle and care for a large pack of hounds, as opposed to individuals. Nevertheless, he wanted advice on the best methods of kenneling such a large number of animals. The Iroquois Hunt had traditionally had between twenty-five and thirty couple of American and crossbred hounds in its kennel. But it was clear to Miller, Mason and Murphy that there were huge differences in the way the sport was carried out in England and in the way hounds were kenneled there. They knew they had much to learn.

So the first in a series of professional hunt servants made his way from England to Lexington in the summer of 1993. Rotating at the rate of one a year, Mickey Wills, John Macey and Philip Stubbings all made an impact at the Iroquois kennel and in Lexington hunting circles.

In their turn, the Englishmen each learned something from the setup in Kentucky. Although General Roger D. Williams's aim in establishing the hunt in the 1880s had reputedly been to provide English-style sport for his friends in the Bluegrass, as has been seen, the club had never slavishly imitated the customs of the English. The hunting had always been given a Kentuckian twist. All subsequent Masters at Iroquois had followed this dictum, and Miller was no exception, perhaps taking it farther than anyone since Williams.

Over time, Miller incorporated radios, road whips, tracking collars and GPS systems into the day-to-day running of the hunt—none of which were familiar in English hunting. And in 1995, Miller conducted a thorough survey of the optimal type of food for the hounds, leading him to the conclusion that dry food, and not the English practice of feeding flesh, was ideal. In this the hunt had come full circle. In 1905, the year of the Great Hound Match, Williams published his thoughts on hunting in his book, *Horse and Hound*, in which he explained his theory of feeding foxhounds: "I have owned a pack of hounds for a quarter of a century and have yet to feed them the carcass of any animal. In winter they are fed one-third cornmeal (unbolted), one-third hog cracklings, and one-third wheat bran. The food is baked as hard as possible, thus forcing them to chew it up. The constant feeding of soft, sloppy, starchy foods, while fattening, leaves the hounds soft and flabby."

Innovation and Conservation

While Miller stayed in place, concentrating his attention on the hound program, the cast of personnel surrounding him changed constantly. Kennel huntsmen from England came and went, as did kennel managers, whippers-in and field masters. There were several changes in the Mastership, too. After the first season with four Masters (1993–94), Bob Brewer resigned and took on the role of honorary secretary. Two seasons later, Jake Graves and Edith Conyers also left. But in 1997, a second Master was elected to serve alongside Jerry Miller, and this time the partnership would stick.

Jack van Nagell was a successful cancer surgeon at the University of Kentucky hospital. He had grown up with a good knowledge of hunting, as his family kept a pack of beagles, but he had never tried mounted foxhunting. As he joked later, "I started riding with the Iroquois because my wife and daughter were so involved with it and I realized that if I ever wanted to see them, I'd better start, too." Miller's and van Nagell's paths at the club mirrored each other precisely—they had joined at the same time, they had received their colors at the end of the same season and they both had been appointed whippers-in.

The two Masters quickly decided to divide up the areas of responsibility so that Miller could continue to focus almost exclusively on the hounds. Van Nagell turned his attention to land, concentrating in particular on conservation. In this, he was following in the footsteps of the first Master, General Roger D. Williams, who, as a charter member of the Boone and Crockett Club and a staunch supporter of Theodore Roosevelt, had been in the vanguard of the nation's efforts to preserve its land and wildlife. Van Nagell was also continuing the work of Fauntleroy Pursley. Like Pursley, van Nagell stressed that without land, the other two elements of the hunt—the hounds and people—went for naught. And increasingly, the land was at risk of development.

In 1927, then Masters Len Shouse and Kendall McDowell had been invited by the farmers around Athens to hunt across their land. But with the purchase of the mill a year later, and the increasing importance of the Pursley family, the center of the hunt country had moved slightly to the south. The Pursleys owned large tracts of land along the east side of the Athens-Boonesboro Road as it wound its way south of Athens and down to the Kentucky River. In the late 1980s and early 1990s, however, the land on the west side of the road started to be developed, and houses and subdivisions started to appear along Combs Ferry Road, too, as Lexington started to spread outward at a rapid rate. More houses meant less land across which the hunt could ride, and more people meant busier roads, putting hounds, horses and riders at greater risk.

And a second factor was also in play. The influx of coyotes into the hunt country had prompted not just a change of hounds but also a different, more direct, style of hunting. Whereas foxes often run in wide circles, making it possible for foxhunters to stay in one place and let the hunt revolve around them, coyotes run straight. In the days of Joe Johnson and Rudolph Singleton and all the way through to the time of Fauntleroy Pursley and Pat Murphy, it had been possible to let the hounds run through the cliffs and gorges of the land near the mill and the creek while the hunters remained on top of a hill to listen to their cry. Now, with coyotes replacing the foxes, the hounds would pick up the scent and be gone in a few seconds. If their safety was to be ensured, the Iroquois Masters and huntsmen would need to stay with them as they ran—something that was almost impossible in the difficult terrain around the mill. Ironically, the arrival of the coyote had created a type of hunting as close to the English style as Iroquois had ever come.

The cumulative effect of these changes—development and new game—was to push the epicenter of the hunt country north again and away from the river. Athens, once again, became the hub. But if the land there was going to be hunted, new relationships would have to be forged and new country opened up. Jack and Betsy van Nagell led the way by purchasing a four-hundred-acre farm, Boone Valley. Miller, for his part, spent long hours in the little country store at Athens, as Pursley had done for so many years at Hazlewood's Store,[84] speaking to the farmers about their concerns, letting them get to know him, assessing the likelihood of being able to put jumps on individuals' properties and reassuring them of the hunt's intention to immediately fix any damage it caused. Together, Miller and van Nagell persuaded a number of landowners to put their acres into conservation easements, and in time, van Nagell's daughter, Knox Pfister, became a leading spokesperson for the Bluegrass's efforts to protect its rural heritage and prevent further development on green field sites. And in 2005, Iroquois's contribution to conservation was recognized when the club won the Mater of Foxhounds Association's Hunting Habitat Conservation Award.

The inevitability of chasing coyotes also prompted many of the innovations Miller introduced at that time. The radios had first been introduced in the late '80s to help Miller and Mason stay in touch with the hounds' progress, principally to aid their own enjoyment. Now they were incorporated as vital pieces of equipment for all whippers-in in order to protect the hounds' safety. On hunt days, the kennel manager, Michael Edwards, was tasked with patrolling the roads in his truck to pick up any errant hounds and to alert the hunt staff if the pack got too close to the roads. And as an additional precaution, the hounds were fitted with tracking collars. Later, with kennel assistant Alan Foy's help, they would be tracked using GPS. These were ideas Miller had formulated from his experiences of night hunting and field trialing. Despite the increasingly English tone of the formal hunt days, the Iroquois Hunt continued to do what it had always done: blend American and English hunting methods into something uniquely its own. The hunt had returned to Athens. A line could be drawn from Roger Williams to Jerry Miller that marked along its route the contributions of Leonard Shouse, Joseph Johnson, Ed Spears and Fauntleroy Pursley. In reality, they weren't that different. Things had never really changed.

Chapter 8

Legacy

One day in 1998, as the hounds were being unboxed at The Corners, Miller crossed the pasture to where Lilla Mason sat on her horse awaiting the start of the hunt. Tossing her his hunting horn, he said casually to Philip Stubbings, his English assistant, "I think we'll let Lilla hunt the hounds today, Philip." Stubbings nodded, and as Miller strode away, Mason realized there was nothing to do but to take up the challenge. With no time for nerves, she blew a sharp note on the horn to tell the hounds it was time for work and tapped her horse into a purposeful trot. As she remembered it later, "It was a total shock, but I saw them both smile, and I thought, 'I'll be danged if I let them get the better of me!' The day sort of snowballed from there, but nothing went too badly wrong."

It might have been a shock, but it was one for which she had, unknowingly, been well prepared. Mason had accompanied Miller on all his tours through Europe and North America. Often, she had sat quietly in the corner of a tack room, in clothes still muddied and damp from the day's hunting, while Miller and some of the most knowledgeable people in the foxhunting world spent long hours discussing the intricacies of the chase and hound breeding. Miller had ensured that Mason had been to field trials and hound shows and that she had hunted behind the most respected huntsmen and whipped in to Iroquois for the previous five years. And over the past few seasons, he had been carefully assembling a pack of hounds he thought would play to Mason's strengths, a style of hunting he knew would be quiet, patient and thoughtful. The years of planning were to pay an ample dividend; over the next ten seasons, Iroquois was to enjoy some of the most exhilarating sport in its history.

At first, Mason would hunt the hounds just a few times a season. Gradually, though, it dawned on her that Miller might actually be intending to hand her the horn permanently. It was something he had intended from the start. "I always knew Lilla would succeed me," he was to say later. "She just had all the natural ability in the world."

To Mason, the idea of replacing Miller seemed a daunting one. Where he was forceful and opinionated, never frightened to let people know if standards were not being met, she was reserved and preferred to avoid confrontation. It was true he had created a pack of hounds to rival any in the world. But the hounds were his. When she rode too close to Miller at the meet, the pack would instinctively stay with him, rather than follow her. They were used to his commands and the sound of his horn.

The hound she was most nervous about was called Grundy. "Grundy was Jerry's hound," Mason explained. "When Jerry was away, I would never take Grundy out. It would be like driving your dad's Porsche. But if Jerry was here and said I could take him, I'd spend the whole day just following him. He was such a professional. I'd just look to see where he was and go there!"

Iroquois Grundy '98 proved to be the foxhound par excellence, the one out of hundreds whose portrait would adorn Miller's desk at AAA. Named by his puppy walker in England after the racehorse that won the 1975 Epsom Derby (the same race Iroquois won in 1881), Grundy was not just a superb hunter—the legend grew up that he would always dispatch a coyote on Miller's birthday—he proved to be a hugely influential sire and a champion in the show ring. Naturally enough, he was of the Carlow ST line and had come from Fanshawe's old hunt, the North Cotswold, courtesy of the new Master there, Nigel Peel.

As Mason recalled:

> *Grundy really changed the whole pack completely because he was a non-switcher. Often, when you hunt coyotes, there'll be several of them. One will go off one way, and another in some different direction. And the hounds can split—say ten couple will go after one and three couple after another—which is something you always want to avoid. But if Grundy started to hunt the trail of one coyote, he would stay on it, and nothing would make him change. And he passed that on to every single one of his progeny.*

Hounds like Peter and Grundy left as important a mark at Iroquois as any Master or huntsman; caring for them when they could no longer hunt would, in turn, become the Iroquois Hunt Club's greatest legacy.

While the two Masters concentrated on their areas of greatest interest—Miller with his hound breeding and van Nagell with the land—the third member of the group, Mason, focused her energies on quietly fomenting a revolution.

In March 2000, Mason and two friends, Glenye Cain and Uschi Graham, signed the paperwork to create the hunting world's first charity dedicated to the care of retired hounds. The Hound Welfare Fund, as the organization was known, aimed to ensure that every hound born at Iroquois was given a home for life, regardless of whether it was able to hunt.

For years, Miller had retired hounds at his own expense. The practice came from his days in Oak Hill, where many people had kept a couple of hounds to take night hunting at weekends. As he reflected later, "Where I grew up, your hounds were not quite part of your family, but close." But within the mounted foxhunting establishments of England, Ireland and the United States, where hunts kept dozens and often scores of hounds, the thought of retiring the old, the injured or the simply untalented was bizarre. In the first place, the argument ran, there was no room. In the second place, there was no money. And in the third place, hounds cannot be retired; they simply aren't happy if they can't hunt. Miller had already shown that hounds could be successfully and happily retired. It was true that the Iroquois retirees had plenty of acres to roam.[85] But they didn't pine on days when their old comrades were taken out and they were left at home. Mason and her friends set about proving that if the desire was there, the money would follow.

Things got off to a shaky start. At Iroquois, some members were slow to see the need for it, and as news spread of the fund's existence, Miller found himself in the firing line from some Masters of other hunts at meetings of the Masters of Foxhounds Association. Within Iroquois and the wider hunting world, there was a concern that drawing attention to the treatment some hounds received at the hands of the huntsmen and Masters they served would bring foxhunting into disrepute. It was far better, many felt, to let sleeping dogs lie.

Gradually, however, the club began to respond. Miller's policy of educating the Iroquois membership had always included asking members to ride as close as they could to the huntsman and the hounds, and prizes were awarded to people who could name the most hounds. In this way, hunting members got to know individual hounds and came to love them. Social members were supportive, too. And the whippers-in, including Herman and Elizabeth Playforth, Blaine Holloway, Hannah Emig and Cecilia Campbell Bowers—all of whom spent many hours with the hounds during the winter and also helped exercise them in the summer—were determined to see the project succeed. And from the start, the fund had enjoyed the unwavering support of three influential members of the hunt: Hilary Boone, Lucy Breathitt and Betsy van Nagell.[86] Together, over the next fifteen years, this group continued to emphasize the ethical importance of giving the Iroquois hounds a secure retirement, and the members embraced the idea.

Under Mason's leadership, and with the staunch support of many Iroquois members, the Hound Welfare Fund prospered, and the retired hounds became ambassadors for the hunt, acting as blood donors to veterinary clinics, being paraded before the start of events at the Kentucky Horse Park and representing the Iroquois pack at the annual Blessing of the Hounds ceremony. The annual fundraiser for the hounds became the club's main social event of the summer. And across the country, other hunts started to consider the idea as younger Masters took charge and foxhunters started to question the traditions of the past. It has, perhaps, become Iroquois's legacy to the world of foxhunting.

Conclusion

Having arrived at the present day, and the end of this brief history, are there any general conclusions that can be drawn about the Iroquois Hunt and the men and women who shaped it? First, it should be re-emphasized that a short supply of both time and space have prevented the inclusion of many of the personalities (and some of the events) that have made Iroquois such a lively, interesting and attractive place. Much more could be said about characters such as Sam Wooldridge (who materially helped Len Shouse with the first pack of hounds in 1926) and families such as the Rankins (Iroquois members and prominent physicians, including a president of the American Medical Association). Indeed, themes such as the strong link between the club and Lexington's medical profession, as well as the role of women and the military in the club's history, merit more research than has been possible. The dedication and enthusiasm shown by the members of the club in the 1920s over events such as the Horse and Hound show, for which Colonel and Mrs. Haggin made an Iroquois Hunt flag, for example, and the work of

Arnold Hanger in preparing the hunt country warrant greater recognition. And little-remembered Lexington figures like Waxey, Herman Trost and the dance-phobic Reverend Robert T. Mathews deserve more than the passing mention they have received. Hopefully, then, this book can spark the interest of historically minded Iroquois members who are in a position to write more about this extraordinary institution and the people who belong to it.

Second, it seems true to say that throughout the course of its 134-year history, the Iroquois Hunt Club has remained true to the original aims and beliefs of its founder of whom General Henry Allen said, "Individuals possessed of such virility and magnetism are born at rare intervals." The club Williams and his friends founded in 1880 (or thereabouts) was not formed in isolation. The period from 1880 to 1930 saw the rise of America's obsession with sport and the creation of thousands of sporting and social clubs. The cause for this phenomenon is sometimes given as a desire to create small communities in the face of increasingly large-scale cities and towns. It is an interesting theory, but one to which Iroquois resolutely does not conform. From the start, the club was always outward-looking; it was never simply a haven in which a small group of rich Bluegrass aristocrats could insulate themselves. Instead, its members were always eager to be involved in the life of the town. And to a significant degree, the members helped create the town in which they lived. Certainly, the focus has narrowed somewhat over the years. As one Master succinctly explained, "The exigencies of modern life and having to earn a living make it impossible for people like General Williams to exist today." And he is no doubt right, considering that in the course of one lifetime, Williams was the owner and manager of two successful businesses, a brigadier general in the Kentucky National Guard and the U.S. Army, an actor, an author, a prospector, a huntsman, a civic leader and a politician. But while the emphasis is now almost exclusively on foxhunting, the club Williams founded continues to participate in the life of the community. Race meets and polo might have gone, but the parade of hounds at the Horse Park and Blessing Day continue.

Williams himself—about whom an entire biography could be produced—is a difficult personality to pin down; he was, to say the least, a multifaceted character. But perhaps at heart he can be defined by four all-consuming passions: entertainment, innovation, conservation and hounds. The men and women who succeeded him at the helm of the Iroquois Hunt—many of whom are descended from the friends who supported his club in the 1880s and 1890s—have tried hard to live up to his example. They have provided Lexington and the Bluegrass with a dazzling array of entertainment, from the annual Blessing Day ceremony and foxhunting to polo, steeplechasing and Keeneland's world-class racing. They have protected the traditions of an ancient sport, preserved a historic building and helped to conserve thousands of acres of the most beautiful land in America. Above all, they have cared for the animals that have served them so well in providing wonderful sport, and they have found new ways to promote their well-being. In this, the Iroquois Hunt Club is doing what it always has—setting a standard for others to match.

Appendix A

List of Masters of the Iroquois Hunt Club

1880–1914: General Roger D. Williams
1926–28: Leonard B. Shouse, Sr., C. Kendall McDowell
1928–30: W. Arnold Hanger, William McDowell
1931–39: Edward F. Spears
1940–70: Edward F. Spears, W. Fauntleroy Pursley
1971–83: W. Fauntleroy Pursley, James Allen
1983–85: Joan Pursley Mayer, William Sphar, James B. Holloway
1986–87: Joan Pursley Mayer, William Sphar
1988–93: Joan Pursley Mayer, Robert Brewer, Jacob H. Graves III
1993–96: Jacob H. Graves, Robert Brewer, Edith Conyers, Jerry L. Miller
1997–2013: Jerry L. Miller, Jack van Nagell Jr.
2014–present: Jerry L. Miller, Jack van Nagell Jr., Lilla S. Mason

Appendix B

List of Huntsmen of the Iroquois Hunt Club

1880–1914: General Roger D. Williams, MFH
1926–27: Bonnie Stone
1927–28: Captain Walter Hall
1928–30: Joe Johnson
1930–32: Rudolph Singleton
1933–68: Edward F. Spears, MFH, and W. Fauntleroy Pursley, MFH
1969–92: Pat Murphy
1992–2000: Jerry L. Miller, MFH
2001–present: Lilla S. Mason, MFH

Glossary of Hunting Terms

all on: Used when all the hounds taken out on a given day are accounted for or present.

buttons: Buttons have a uniquely important significance in hunting. To refer to someone being given their "hunt buttons" means they have been invited to wear the hunt's insignia and indicates a level of acceptance or admittance into the hunt family. In America, this is more often referred to as being "awarded one's colors" and allows the conferee to wear the hunt's color on the collar of his or her hunt coat. However, the number of buttons worn on a hunt coat can also indicate a specific role within the hunt, with hunt staff being allowed to wear more buttons than members of the field so that they can be easily distinguished.

cast: The huntsman instructs the hounds to spread out to search for a line of the fox.

check: A pause in the hunt caused by hounds losing the line of the fox.

colors: See "buttons."

country: The area of land designated as belonging to a specific hunt.

couple: All hounds are counted in couples, even when there are odd numbers (e.g. fifteen hounds would be referred to as seven and a half couple. (N.B. Couple can also refer to a leather leash for keeping two hounds attached and which is used for training the hounds.)

covert (pronounced "cover"): A wooded area where a fox or coyote might be found.

cry (also "speak" and "give tongue"): Refers to the various sounds made by hounds when they are hunting.

cub hunting (also "cubbing" and "autumn hunting"): Hunting before the start of the formal season, which is used to train young hounds. It is usually conducted at a slower pace and earlier in the day than formal hunting.

drag hunting: Hunting in which hounds follow the line of an artificial scent, rather than pursue a live quarry.

draw: To search for a fox or coyote in a covert.

entered hound: A hound that has been hunted for one season or more.

field: The people who follow the hunt, excluding the Masters and hunt staff.

field master: The person in charge of the field while out hunting.

fixture card: The schedule of dates and times of meets, usually printed on a card and sent to members of the hunt at the beginning of the season.

hill-topping: Can refer either to those who follow the hunt at a greater distance than the rest of the field and who do not jump or to the practice of congregating on top of a hill to listen to the hounds work rather than physically following them to watch them work.

huntsman: Can be either amateur (in which case he or she is almost invariably also a Master) or professional. The person who directs and controls the hounds and the hunt once a hunt starts through the use of voice commands and a hunting horn. (Only the huntsman uses a horn during a hunt.) The huntsman is also responsible for the kennel and for the hounds' welfare, training and daily routine.

kennel huntsman: If the Master hunts the hounds, a professional is usually employed to look after hounds in the kennel.

lift: To collect the hounds and instruct them to start searching for the fox in a new place.

line: The route taken by the hunted fox or coyote.

Master (Master of Foxhounds, MFH): The person in charge of the hunt with overall responsibility for the hounds. The Master is also responsible for the country through liaising with landowners. N.B. The term "Master" is gender non-specific. A female Master is not called a mistress!

meet: The place designated for the hunt to assemble before the start of a hunt.

nose: The ability of a hound to detect the scent of the hunted fox or coyote.

panel: A jump built into a fence line.

scent: The smell of the fox or coyote—believed to be left by the animal's footprints—that is sensed by the hounds.

staff: Collective term for the huntsman and whippers-in.

stern: The tail of a hound.

unbox: Hounds are usually taken to a meet in some kind of conveyance, so when they are turned out ready for the hunt, it is referred to as "unboxing the hounds."

voice: The quality of a hound's cry. It can be deep, soft, melodious, sharp, etc.

whippers-in (whip): The staff members who assist the huntsman in controlling the hounds out hunting.

Notes

Introduction

1. Millnor, *Memoirs*.
2. Howe, "Fox Hunting as Ritual."

Chapter 1

3. *Kentucky Leader*, July 7, 1889.
4. Ibid.
5. Ibid., January 28, 1894.
6. Pierre Lorillard IV (1833–1901), American tobacco manufacturer and Thoroughbred racehorse breeder.
7. First run in 1780, by the 1880s, the Derby was the most important race on the equine sporting calendar. Lexington's newspapers regularly reported the racing from England and particularly from Epsom, where the Derby is still run. When news of Iroquois's victory at Epsom filtered through to America, business stopped on Wall Street completely, and a ticker-tape parade was organized. The day after the race, the *New York Times* ran a front-page story listing the prominent Americans who had been lucky enough to witness the victory in person.
8. Herman Trost (1836–1923), founder of the first marching band at the University of Kentucky. Trost was part of a group of immigrants from Germany and Prussia known as the Forty-Eighters, who had participated in or supported the European revolutions of 1848. Trost was a close

friend of John Philip Sousa and had been a bandleader in Sherman's army during the Civil War. He founded many bands and orchestras in Lexington throughout the period.

9. *Lexington Herald*, December 13, 1925.
10. *Illustrated History of Nebraska*, vol. II, 615.
11. The original Roger Williams left England in 1630 to escape the corruption of the Church of England, into which he had been ordained after leaving Pembroke College, Cambridge. Unfortunately, he found a similar state of corruption in America. After being invited to preach at, and subsequently quarreling with, a dizzying array of churches, Roger Williams eventually settled in Providence. He was a proponent of peaceful co-existence with the Native American people and an outspoken opponent of slavery, an attitude that has earned him a great deal of admiration retrospectively but that made him a figure of grave suspicion at the time.
12. *Lexington Herald*, December 13, 1925.
13. The Black Hills continued to exercise a powerful hold on Williams for the rest of his life. Fifty years later, in 1925, he was invited back to Deadwood as one of the few surviving 75ers, the people who had prospected for gold in the Black Hills in the mid-1870s.
14. "[Crawford's] first scouting duty was as chief of scouts for the Black Hills Rangers…and his lieutenant was a Kentucky youngster named Roger D. Williams." *Illustrated History of Nebraska*, vol. II, 615.
15. John Wallace Crawford (1847–1917), journalist, performer, explorer and adventurer known as the "Poet Scout," became a national celebrity after riding 350 miles in six days while carrying dispatches for the *New York Herald* telling of the victory of General Crook at the Battle of Slim Buttes during the Great Sioux War of 1876–77.
16. McLaird, *Calamity Jane*, 46.
17. Edwin Booth (1833–1893) of the Anglo-American Booth acting dynasty. Booth was credited with developing a more naturalistic acting style than that of his father, Junius Brutus Booth, and his father's contemporary Edmund Keen. In a bizarre coincidence, Edwin Booth is reputed to have saved the life of Abraham Lincoln's son, Robert, at a train station in New Jersey a few weeks before Booth's brother, John Wilkes Booth, assassinated the president.
18. Johnson, *History of Kentucky and Kentuckians*, 1613–14.
19. U.S. Bureau of the Census, Population of the 100 Largest Urban Places: 1880.
20. Hollingsworth, *Lexington*, 124.
21. Ibid.

22. The Van Meters, like many landowners in Lexington, were closely involved with breeding livestock. At that time, Kentucky was as famous for its pedigree cattle and sheep as it was for Thoroughbreds and hounds, with many prize breeding specimens being imported from England.
23. When they weren't engaged for a special social occasion, Waxey and his band would play in the corridors of the local hotels. When Waxey died in April 1894 at just thirty years old, his obituary in the *Kentucky Leader* noted, "Waxey was leader of a band of musicians and jubilee singers that made a tour of the United States and Canada and also went to Europe with the original Uncle Tom's Cabin Company. He will be continually missed by thousands of people whom he has entertained."
24. The Gentry family is descended from "Richard Gentry, a soldier of the Revolutionary War who lies buried at Crab Orchard Springs." In 1899, the General organized a huge gathering of the Gentry clan that was widely reported in the Lexington press. Over one hundred descendants of Richard Gentry from eight states made their way to Crab Orchard, where the General had arranged food and sporting entertainment for all. Seven years later, he did the same thing again. Whether the General was simply in touch with the zeitgeist or had an individual mania for reunions is difficult to say. But in his zeal, he did not draw the line just at reuniting the Gentry diaspora. In 1907, he agitated successfully for Kentucky to send a delegation to the disastrous Jamestown Exposition, an event that marked the tercentenary of Christopher Newport's first landing in Virginia (though it was held in Norfolk) and resulted in huge financial losses for the promoters due to poor attendance.
25. *Kentucky Leader*, August 4, 1899.
26. Madeleine McDowell Breckinridge (1872–1920), vice-president of the National Woman Suffrage Association, founder of the Lexington Civic League and proponent of the League of Nations.

Chapter 2

27. In *Bluegrass and Rhododendron*, John Fox records one young Kentuckian telling him of a foxhound that had been on a hunt lasting over twenty hours.
28. According to John Fox, the Walkers would hunt three nights a week all year round, with May being considered the best month.
29. Williams enjoyed his finest moment as a field trialer at La Grange, Kentucky, in November 1913, when his hound Phill won the Hunting and Trailing section of the National All Age Futurity Championship.
30. Little has occurred to disturb the basic format of field trialing over the intervening 120 years. The hounds of every sportsman wishing to take part

have identifying numerals painted on their sides. At daybreak, or just after, all the hounds are released simultaneously. And there is no dawdling around waiting for instructions from the huntsman, as is seen at the average English hunt. Instead, the hounds disappear into the darkness, and it is up to the judges, who roam the surrounding country on horseback, to see which hounds work best. They must be meticulous in their record keeping. For example: "At 7:30 a.m., I saw hound 642 asleep under a tree." The trial lasts on average five hours, and then, while the judges confer about the scores, the hounds' owners frantically try to retrieve their animals, as hounds that are not back within twenty-four hours are disqualified.

31. Olympian Springs (originally known as Mud Lick Springs) was purchased by Colonel Thomas Hart, Henry Clay's father-in-law, in the early nineteenth century. Hart built a hotel on the property, and the site quickly became a fashionable health spa. In 1803, the first stagecoach route in Kentucky was established between Olympian Springs and Lexington. One story says that Henry Clay took over the ownership of the resort and lost it in a game of poker.

32. Rookwood Kennels was a serious business, importing all types of hunting dogs, including wolfhounds, bear hounds, foxhounds, bloodhounds and deer hounds from England, Ireland, Russia, France and Norway. Each year, a booklet would be produced detailing the stud fees of the various hounds at the kennel and also giving the prices for procuring different types of hound. Rookwood's results at field trials and bench shows across the country were crucial to its success and widely advertised.

33. Noel Mullins, *Foxhunting Life*.

34. Glenye Cain Oakford, Full Cry: A Hound Blog.

35. It should be noted that the Camargo Hunt of Cincinnati favored English hounds. It was a definite choice on the part of the Iroquois Hunt's officers to have Walker hounds and not simply a matter of using whatever hounds were closest to hand.

Chapter 3

36. There are, in fact, two different versions of the General's whereabouts on the evening before he died. The official account, given in the newspapers the following day, stated that he was at the theater. However, it is popularly believed—including by the General's descendants—that he was at a brothel. However, it was not Belle Brezing's establishment, as Brezing's house had closed fifteen years earlier. When it was open, it had been on the same street as the General's iron foundry, now Thoroughbred Park in downtown Lexington.

37. Major General Henry Tureman Allen (1859–1930) was a noted explorer and the general officer who arranged for Roger Williams to serve in France in 1918. An enthusiastic foxhunter, Allen was Master of the Coblenz Hunt Club, which provided sport for the Army of Occupation on the Rhine after the end of the war. Hounds were drafted from America, England and France, and "the hunts were always held in a mostly wooded section in the foothills on the east bank of the Rhine about ten miles from Coblenz," according to a young officer, Joseph Magoffin Glasgow.
38. Lieutenant Colonel Georges Thenault (1887–1948) commanded the French Escadrille, a unit of the French Armeé de l'Air in World War I composed of volunteer American pilots.
39. Lexington's army officers would be staunch supporters of the club when it was eventually re-founded. Captain Frank Wright was a whipper-in until his untimely death in 1928, and Captain William Armstrong, formerly the riding instructor at Culver Military Academy, would "help significantly in teaching the lady members the art of riding to hounds." In an additional gesture of support, the Cavalry Club allowed its room to be used as an early headquarters for the new club and also helped to build a stable near the remount depot for use in stabling Iroquois members' horses, known as the hunt's "town stables." And the Army's Remount Section also provided members with horses for many of the hunts in the first few years of the new club's existence. (Remounts are young horses that have been fairly well broken, but not at all trained. More experienced mounts were offered to Iroquois members, but as Charlotte Pursley was to recall in 2002, "Those cavalry horses still took some handling.")
40. The two-week hiatus between the paper chase and the first drag hunt was not simply the club proceeding cautiously. Nor was it to allow time to acquire hounds and find a venue. In fact, it was to let members attend the annual Lexington race meet—then as now, nothing could be done while the races were on.
41. Ernest Whitworth Marland (1874–1941) eventually became governor of Oklahoma despite, or perhaps because of, shocking his constituents' moral sensibilities by marrying his adopted daughter, Lydie, following the death of his first wife.
42. The drag hunt was to be kenneled separately at Hamburg Place and consisted of five couple of Walker hounds.
43. The phrase "according to Hoyle" refers to Edmund Hoyle (1672–1769), who wrote extensively on the rules of card games. The phrase was expanded to refer in general to any putative authority.
44. Founded in 1926 in Louisville, the Muldraugh Hunt's first president was General Ellerbe Carter, and the huntsman was Baylor Hickman. The

hunt's country consisted of ten thousand acres of Camp Knox, and the officers' club was the hunt's headquarters. The Muldraugh had a pack of Walker hounds.

45. To panel the country meant to put in jumps over which the riders could cross, most fields being divided by wire, which is difficult and dangerous to jump. Installing and maintain jumps was, and is still, the responsibility of the Masters. As J.B. Thomas indicated, it is an extremely laborious and expensive business.

46. The Old Duke's wealth was based almost entirely on slavery; he owned the largest number of slaves in the town (and according to some sources the largest number in the state). Lexington was a hub of the slave trade and home to an infamous market where thousands of people were sold. English author Anthony Trollope observed slavery firsthand when he stayed on a stock farm near Lexington during his visit to the town in early 1862. Despite adopting a deplorably casual attitude to one of the worst injustices in modern history, Trollope did provide an intriguing insight into various aspects of how Kentuckian slave owners viewed the matter: "A gentleman in Kentucky does not sell his slaves. To do so is considered to be low and mean, and is opposed to the aristocratic traditions of the country. A man who does so willingly, puts himself beyond the pale of good-fellowship with his neighbours. A sale of slaves is regarded as a sign almost of bankruptcy. If a man cannot pay his debts, his creditors can step in and sell his slaves; but he does not himself make the sale." A. Trollope, *North America* (London: Chapman and Hall, 1862).

47. Colonel E.R. Bradley's famous Kentucky Derby winner was named Burgoo King for James Looney.

48. The Mason & Hanger Company helped create, among other things, the Grand Coulee Dam, the Lincoln Tunnel and the Nevada nuclear test site.

49. Sterling Loop Larrabee (1889–1974) entered West Point in 1908 before joining the Philippine Constabulary for two years. He served in the British navy and British army in World War I, being severely wounded at Gallipoli and subsequently serving with the American artillery after 1917. After the war, he settled in Virginia and established a private pack. He was married twice, first to Madge Stokes Stone, owner of the Oakwood estate in Virginia, and then to the famous British photographer Constance Stuart Larrabee.

50. Overhills was an eleven-thousand-acre sporting estate abutting Fort Bragg near Pinehurst, North Carolina, purchased by the Rockefeller family in the early 1900s. In the '20s, Percy Rockefeller, Averell Harriman and George Walker each built houses on the estate in order to pursue their sporting interests: foxhunting (Rockefeller), bird hunting (Harriman)

and golfing (Walker). American architect, author and foxhunter Joseph B. Thomas would take his hounds from New York and Virginia to Overhills for two months each season, and Rockefeller and his guests would hunt with him. The complex included a fully equipped stable and kennel for the hunt horses and hounds, as well as a huntsman's house. Like the guests, the hounds would arrive by train, brought by Thomas's huntsman, Charles Carver.

Chapter 4

51. It is assumed that General Williams and Bonnie Stone hunted south of the town in the area around Athens because that is where Rookwood Kennels was located. However, there are apparently no contemporaneous documentary accounts to confirm this, only the reference in *The Chase* dated 1927.
52. The 1904 map shows the location of the kennel (still at Athens) and the hunt's town stables (on Richmond Road). It also lists the names of every landowner in the area, many of whose families had owned and farmed the land for generations. Many of the names are familiar to Iroquois members today, either because the families are still there or because coverts and landmarks are known by the names of the family, such as Smitha's Cliff.
53. Gourlay, originally from Melrose, Scotland, immigrated to the United States in 1910 at the age of twenty-one. He had trained as a civil engineer and headed to the California oilfields, arriving just in time for the largest spill in history. In Santa Maria, he met Attilia Bonetti, daughter of millionaire oilman and landowner John Bonetti. They married, and when he was appointed general manager of a subsidiary of the Superior Oil Corporation in 1920, they moved to Lexington, living at 9 Mentelle Park. Gourlay was an accomplished artist, decorating many of the club's early invitation cards with humorous foxhunting scenes. In 1929, J.B. Thomas asked him to become the manager of Grasslands, a twenty-eight-square-mile tract of land near Gallatin, Tennessee, which Thomas and three investors hoped to turn into a sporting paradise for millionaires. Membership started at $10,000, and every conceivable activity was catered for: beagling, foxhunting, dove and quail shooting, fishing and golfing. The centerpiece was a four-and-a-half-mile steeplechase course modeled on Aintree in England, the home of the Grand National. The first race was held on May 19, 1930, and a crowd of 8,000 watched the Iroquois Hunt's whipper-in Byron Hilliard win on Red Gold; Hilliard's stepfather, Barry Bingham (owner of the *Louisville Courier-Journal*), ensured plenty of newspaper column inches were devoted to the event. The evening before the race, a masked

ball for 350 guests was held at the local mansion. Ladies were invited to wear powdered wigs and antebellum costumes, while the gentlemen donned their scarlet hunting tailcoats. So many East Coast socialites attended that the party was featured in *Vogue*. Naturally, after such a promising start, the whole thing went hideously wrong, and in 1932, Grasslands was put into receivership, another victim of the Great Depression.

54. John Winn married into the Dulin family, who were already settled in the area and from whom today's landowner Tommy Dulin of Dulin Farm is descended.

55. In the early years, the food was often served buffet style on tables downstairs. Members would help themselves and then take their plates upstairs and sit on long benches rather than chairs.

Chapter 5

56. The joke went that Iroquois members built St. Hubert's so they could drink all night and then go to church the next day on their way home, presumably to atone for their all-too-recent sins. In the late 1960s, Winnie Morris—formerly Winnie Madden, wife of Ed Madden of Hamburg Place and polo team fame—donated a five-acre tract of land on Grimes Mill Road, next to the lane known as Munch's Corner. Bishop William Moody of the Episcopal Diocese of Lexington provided the drawings for a small stone church, which he had based on the style of an English country church. The building—made of Kentucky limestone and measuring just twenty-five by fifty-five feet—was completed in 1969 and was consecrated on November 3, the Sunday nearest to St. Hubert's feast day.

Iroquois members provided much of the decoration. John Jacob Niles carved the oak doors, taking as his theme the Eighty-Fourth Psalm, "How Lovely Is Your Dwelling Place." Clarence LeBus donated the antique bell that hangs in the freestanding belfry. Cast in 1862, the bell, which is known as "Bell Clarence," was rescued from being melted down during World War II "by being buried in a corn field." And many of the decorations, including the needlepoint kneelers, have hunting-related themes. For fifteen years after its consecration, St. Hubert's remained unaffiliated with the national church or the diocese of Lexington. "Bishop Moody called it a 'peculiar' church, like Westminster Abbey, because it did not belong to any Church body."

57. James Gordon Bennett Jr. (1841–1918), publisher of the *New York Herald* and sponsor of Henry Stanley's expedition to Africa to find David Livingstone. Bennett was noted for his erratic behavior, which included urinating into a grand piano (or possibly a fireplace) in full view of his

putative parents-in-law and their guests. Bennett left for Europe soon after. An enthusiastic sportsman, Bennett was the youngest-ever commodore of the New York Yacht Club and established automobile races, balloon races and the Westchester Polo Club. He also created the *Paris Herald*, forerunner of the *International Herald Tribune*.

58. John Edward Madden (1856–1929), known as the "Wizard of the Turf." Madden grew up in Pennsylvania in a poor household. He amassed a fortune through harness racing before moving into Thoroughbred breeding and racing. His first great success was Hamburg, which he bought as a yearling for $1,200. During his two-year-old season, Hamburg won $38,000, and Madden sold him for another $40,000. The profits funded the purchase of Hamburg Place, from which Madden sent out fourteen champions, including four winners of the Kentucky Derby.

59. Harry Payne Whitney (1872–1930) inherited $24 million from his father in 1904 and $12 million from his uncle in 1917 and married a member of the equally impecunious Vanderbilt family. Whitney was a noted polo player and owner and breeder of polo ponies and Thoroughbreds, coincidentally inheriting from his father the horse Hamburg, formerly owned by John Madden.

60. According to an article in the *Lexington Herald-Leader* of January 11, 1953, the Lexington Polo Club "never grew out of infancy. The same year it was conceived, most of its members left in a dispute over polo club policy and formed the new group that was to become [the] Iroquois [polo team]."

61. No. 1 field, where the major games were played, was regulation size (300 yards by 160 yards), while Nos. 2 and 3 were slightly smaller and used for practice and children's matches.

62. It is often specified that Bluegrass originated on the steppes near the Black Sea and was brought by Mennonite immigrants, but the genus is indigenous to many parts of Europe and Asia.

63. Many early settlements in Kentucky had Race Streets, which were usually straight and wide and named for the obvious reason that that was where races were held.

64. Rena Niles was a journalist and the wife of John Jacob Niles (1892–1980), the American composer, singer and collector of traditional ballads who was known as the "Dean of American Balladeers." John Jacob Niles had a profound effect on the American folk music of the 1950s. He was famous among members of the hunt for playing the Appalachian dulcimer, which many found to be an acquired taste.

65. When Spears was first elected Master, the pack consisted of ten couple of Walker hounds and ten couple of Bywaters; by the time Pursley became joint-Master in 1940, they were all Walkers.

Chapter 6

66. The show was not held between 1942 and 1946.
67. The 1929 Roger Williams Memorial Trophy was won by Arnold Hanger. In 1953, to mark the twenty-fifth anniversary of his victory, Hanger donated an antique silver bowl to be presented each year to the winner.
68. Anyone who has witnessed the comparative orderliness of American and English people standing in line will know that the susceptibility is not confined to hounds.
69. A couple is a pair of leather collars connected to each other by a strap and designed to ensure the two dogs go everywhere together. Its effect is to make a younger dog learn correct behavior.
70. In the 1930s, the pack had contained almost an equal number of Walker hounds and Bywater hounds (a legacy of Joe Johnson's two seasons as huntsman). But both types of hound are essentially night-hunting hounds and share the same characteristics, namely independence and individuality.
71. Spears was on his way to a meet. His horse, Smokey, was stabled with Pat Murphy. After the crash, Spears appeared to be only slightly injured and called Pat's wife to explain he had been in a wreck and would be delayed because the hospital doctors wanted to take X-rays. He died the next day.
72. Richard and Tessa Dole founded the Woodford Hounds in 1981. Dick Dole was the former Master of the Mells Foxhounds in Tennessee and the Blue Ridge Hunt in Virginia. They had come to Kentucky in search of good land to hunt over and found ample room in southern Woodford County and western Jessamine County. In 1982, Charlie Walker, an equine veterinarian and a former whipper-in to the Mells Foxhounds, joined Dick and Tessa Dole at Woodford. The connections between the two hunts were strong. Herman Playforth, Jim Holloway's son-in-law, was a Master at Woodford before becoming a whipper-in at Iroquois, and several families are members of both hunts today.

Chapter 7

73. Founded in 1962–63, the Banwen Miners Hunt was, for many years, run by the inhabitants of the small colliery village of Banwen in Wales. When the colliery closed down, its owner gave the miners the old lamp room as their hunt kennels.
74. Iroquois had been supplied with several drafts of hounds from Mose Hill during Joan Mayer's Mastership.
75. The show's correct title is the Mid-America Hound Show.

76. C. Martin Wood III, MFH and Daphne Wood, MFH, of the Live Oak Hounds, Monticello, Florida.
77. Baronet: the holder of a baronetcy, the only hereditary title not to be part of the peerage. Baronets are addressed as "sir," hence "Sir Peter Farquhar."
78. Hounds are named using the first two letters of their dam's name, and when they formally enter the pack and start hunting, they are also given the hunt's name as a prefix and their year of entry as a suffix. For example, the offspring of Iroquois Fiona '01 would all have names beginning with the letters "Fi" and, if entered into the Iroquois pack in 2014, would from then on be known as Iroquois Fi—— '14.
79. Mrs. Olive Hall enjoyed a long reign at the Carlow, starting in the 1920s. A large and imposing figure both physically and personally, she is famously supposed to have remarked to a groom who had the temerity to rebuke her for overtiring her horse: "Sweating? Don't be ridiculous, man! So would you be sweating excessively, if you'd just spent the last five hours lodged between my thighs!" Carlow County, Ireland Genealogical Project.
80. The Carlow ST bloodline is now well represented in many kennels around the world, including the Duke of Beaufort's and the Torrington Farmers in England, the Midland in the United States and the Ellerslie Camperdown Hunt in Australia.
81. While the Cottesmore was unlikely ever to elect a professional huntsman as Master, Neil Coleman did eventually become Master of the Torrington Farmers Hunt in Devon, England, from where he continued to send English hounds to Iroquois.
82. George Stubbs (1724–1806), English artist whose works include *Whistlejacket* and *The Anatomy of the Horse* and who is regarded as the greatest painter of the horse in history.
83. Eventually, the Iroquois Hunt would help to pioneer a successful treatment of the disease, and the kennel manager, Michael Edwards, would become more adept than any veterinary technician in nursing sick hounds suffering from the effects of the infection.
84. Both sets of Masters had taken the responsibility of building relationships with the local landowners and farmers immensely seriously, but it was Pursley who turned it into an art. Whole days were spent visiting the country stores, chewing tobacco and talking about livestock and crops, and Pursley also underwrote many of the loans the farmers needed to purchase supplies until they could sell their produce at market.

Chapter 8

85. In another innovation, and to ensure there was no excess of hounds in the kennel, Miller initiated a policy of breeding only one or two litters of hounds a year at Iroquois.
86. Boone was the president of the club when the Hound Welfare Fund started and was shocked to learn how hounds were often treated elsewhere. Breathitt was a former White House social secretary and wife of one of Kentucky's most beloved governors, Ned Breathitt. Van Nagell, as well as being the wife of Miller's joint-Master, was also one of the hunt's largest and most beneficent landowners.

Selected Bibliography

Clark, Thomas D. *My Century in History*. Lexington: University Press of Kentucky, 2006.

Enoch, Harry G. *Grimes Mill: Kentucky Landmark on Boone Creek, Fayette County*. Berwyn Heights, MD: Heritage Books, 2002.

Fox, John. *Bluegrass and Rhododendron: Outdoors in Old Kentucky*. New York: Charles Scribner's Sons, 1901.

Hollingsworth, Randolph. *Lexington: Queen of the Bluegrass*. Charleston, SC: Arcadia Publishing, 2004.

Howe, James. "Fox Hunting as Ritual." *American Ethnologist* 8, no. 2 (May 1981): 278–300.

Iroquois Hunt Club Papers. Special Collections, M.I. King Library, University of Kentucky.

Johnson, E. Polk. *A History of Kentucky and Kentuckians: The Leaders and Representative Men in Commerce, Industry and Modern Activities*. Vol. 3. New York: Lewis Publishing Company, 1912.

Masters of Foxhounds Association. *A Centennial View: Foxhunting in North America Today*. New York: Derrydale Press, 2009.

McLaird, James D. *Calamity Jane: The Woman and the Legend*. Norman: University of Oklahoma Press, 2005.

Millnor, William, Jr. *Memoirs of the Gloucester Fox Hunting Club Near Philadelphia*. New York: Ernest Gee, 1927.

Williams, Roger D. *The Fox Hound*. New York: Outing Publishing Company, 1914.

———. *Horse and Hound*. Lexington, KY: Williams, 1905.

Index

About the Authors

Christopher and Glenye Oakford are freelance writers with special interests in social history, nature, politics and sport. Christopher grew up in England, where he worked for the United Kingdom's Ministry of Defence. A trained historian, he was responsible for helping identify the remains of fallen British soldiers from World War I and other past wars. Since moving to the United States in 2006, he's been a regular contributor to *Covertside* magazine.

During her twenty-year journalism career, Glenye has covered a variety of horse sports, and her work has appeared in such publications as *Daily Racing Form*, *The Blood-Horse*, ESPN.com and *The Chronicle of the Horse*. She's also the author of *The Home Run Horse*, an entertaining history of the quest for a life-changing champion racehorse. In 2012, she won Thoroughbred racing's Eclipse Award for multimedia work.

The Oakfords live in Lexington, Kentucky, where they recently started a videography business specializing in nonprofit organizations and animal-related topics.